▮▮▮ Return on Learning

Return on Learning

Training for High Performance
at Accenture

DONALD VANTHOURNOUT

KURT OLSON

JOHN CEISEL

ANDREW WHITE

TAD WADDINGTON

THOMAS BARFIELD

SAMIR DESAI

CRAIG MINDRUM

AGATE

CHICAGO

Library of Congress Cataloging-in-Publication Data

Return on Learning : Training for High Performance at Accenture / by Donald Vanthournout ... [et al.].
     p.   cm.
     Summary: "Story of how Accenture, one of the world's most widely known companies, revolutionized its internal corporate training operation"—Provided by publisher.
     ISBN-13: 978-1-932841-18-3 (hardcover)
     ISBN-10: 1-932841-18-0 (hardcover)
     1. Financial services industry—Employees—Training of—United States.
     2. Accenture (Firm) 3. Financial planners—United States. I. Vanthournout, Donald.
     HD5716.F472U66 2006
     658.3'1243—dc22

                                                        2005037141

10 9 8 7 6 5 4 3 2 1

Agate books are available in bulk at discount prices. For more information, go to agatepublishing.com.

CONTENTS

PREFACE

Jill B. Smart
Senior Managing Director, Human Resources, Accenture

The story you are about to read tells how a major global company drove toward high performance by reinventing the way it supported its workforce with learning services, as well as knowledge sharing and collaboration capabilities. At the same time, it is more than just one company's story. It offers lessons for any CEO, COO or CFO who is looking to create competitive advantage today, and it is for that reason we feel bold enough to share our story with others.

Over the past several years, Accenture has experienced a dramatic transformation, spurred by one of the most challenging times in Accenture's history—indeed, in the history of the global economy. Faced with worldwide economic turmoil following the bursting of the Internet bubble, the broad effects of global terrorism, the rapidly changing needs of corporations and governments—our clients—and increased margin pressures, the traditional field of "training" appeared to be a relic of a different era.

The rules of the training game had changed—and changed permanently. No longer was it acceptable simply to train our people to meet short-term, day-to-day needs driven by individual organizational priorities. "Training" that is planned and directed from a central organization would still have an important place; but also important would be the broader "learning" agenda for our people, both directed and self-directed. To be truly viable, enterprise learning programs would now have to meet the long-term, strategic needs of the company.

Above all, no longer would it be acceptable to run learning as a cost center. With budgets shrinking everywhere, one could no longer simply assume that the learning program was "important." Those of us in charge of learning at Accenture had to prove that it added value to the company. Moreover, we had to run the learning function more efficiently and rigorously, with one eye on the bottom line and the other on the value being created for the company.

For executives looking to transform their workforce performance capabilities, Accenture's story presents numerous critical factors. One of the more groundbreaking aspects of this work was a major return on investment study, conducted by our own internal organization, but also validated by leading university professors. Based on this study, we were able to quantify the value of enterprise learning by measuring its impact on recruiting, retention, chargeability and performance. We discovered that for every dollar Accenture invests in learning, the company receives that dollar back plus an additional $3.53 in measurable value to its bottom line—in other words, a 353 percent return on learning. This ROI model won a number of awards, including a Corporate University Xchange award for excellence in measurement, and two awards from the American Society for Training and Development.

Our ROI work was especially important because it got the attention and respect of our most senior executives and helped secure their ongoing support for Accenture's broader transformational change program focused on learning. As we all know, senior executives at any major company or government agency have many things to monitor and manage. Transformation initiatives often falter because the payback does not appear to be important enough to merit attention at the highest level, or because other initiatives come along that appear to be more pressing. Our ROI study made it clear that enterprise learning is a strategic initiative of the highest importance.

The Accenture team also put in place an effective governance structure that was responsible for ensuring consistent support for the transformation of learning. Major organizational change is never easy. But when you have your most senior decision makers sponsoring the overall program and articulating how the organizational changes will help achieve overall business objectives, it can make things easier.

And we cannot forget the quality of the learning experiences themselves. The Accenture team created innovative curricula and courses for the company, and incorporated leading thinking from the industry on how to deliver learning based on new technologies: e-learning, Web-based seminars and knowledge management applications. But we did not forget our roots as a company, either. One of the things that made learning special at Accenture was the centralized courses offered at the main facility Accenture uses in St. Charles, Illinois, just outside of Chicago. This campus was where new hires got to know the special culture of the company and speed their way to competency in a kind of "boot camp" atmosphere. So we went "back to basics" there, renewing our commitment to classroom learning by incorporating it as a central component in much of our revitalized core curriculum program.

At an early stage of this transformational journey, I challenged our core team to make sure that, whatever else we did, we delivered what I called "phenomenal" learning experiences to our people. Anyone glancing through the course evaluation forms for Accenture today will see that we succeeded. Learning at Accenture is changing people's lives; it is giving them more reason than ever to stay with us and grow both personally and professionally. We have successfully aligned our learning strategy with Accenture's business strategy and significantly upgraded our core curricula to meet today's needs in each of Accenture's four workforces. Perhaps most important, we have had a positive impact on the performance of our business.

That is one final thought I want to leave you with: organizations can successfully use learning programs for major business impact, and can run learning like a business. Today, we are helping Accenture advance toward high performance through innovative learning solutions that generate a measurable, positive impact on Accenture's bottom line. We are also delivering important efficiencies, spending more than 40 percent less on learning and development today than five years ago, even as our workforce has grown by 50 percent during that same time.

Please join us now on this journey of a company advancing toward high performance by maximizing its "return on learning." It's a journey that you and your organization can make, as well.

▶ *One*

High Performance through Learning

In a courtyard on the sprawling, 96-acre campus in St. Charles, Illinois, that has been the hub of Accenture's global training organization for more than 30 years, stand two bronze figures. Dressed in the professional business garb that was *de rigeur* for a consulting and professional services organization before the days of "business casual," a young man and woman chat with each other. The man is seated on a bench, a textbook open on his lap, gesturing with one hand; the woman, holding a leather briefcase, bends down to hear what he is saying—both of them captured in time as if they were preparing for another of the rigorous 14- or 16-hour days that can characterize the initial training and orientation period for a new Accenture employee. In fact, if you look closely, the woman's wristwatch reads 8:27: time to get to class.

The enduring presence of these statues has been an important symbol of the company's cultural strength: its ongoing commitment to the development of its people. This is especially so for Accenture's newest hires—some coming in with years of experience, but others just entering the workforce as fresh-faced university graduates who, in the course of just a few months, became walking, talking embodiments of the advanced technology skills and rigorous delivery methodologies that rocketed the firm to the top of the global consulting business.

That commitment, and that extensive training program at Accenture—one that started the very first week on the job and continued at relevant intervals throughout a person's entire career—meant that a client could walk into an Accenture office in Chicago, or London, or Manila, or Buenos Aires or any of Accenture's offices in the 48 countries in which it now operates, and find almost uniform levels of competence among employees and a stable, consistent approach to executing a technology, strategy or outsourcing project. It meant that a client could ask anyone on a project team—the newest hire or the most senior executive—about the purpose and progress of the work and get a good sense of where things stood: what the goals and vision were, what distinctive value was being created, what milestones had been reached, what work remained and how that person's role and tasks fit into the whole.

Good for the client, and good for Accenture, at least as things stood through the late 1990s. Those trained resources, even the newest of them, meant that an incredible amount of high-quality work could be accomplished on time and on budget, at respectable margins. The consulting field was crowded, but Accenture was one of the giants. Not the cheapest management consultant on the block, to be sure. But clients knew that if they had a mission-critical job to accomplish, one that was to be built on the innovative application of advanced technology and business thinking—and if they wanted the project delivered on time and on budget, with less risk—Accenture was the company to turn to.

Training its employees in support of this business model didn't come cheaply to Accenture either. But knowing that its competitive advantage in that crowded consulting marketplace rested on its people, Accenture was prepared to invest heavily: the company's annual spending on employee learning and development had actually topped $700 million in its 2001 fiscal year. More than they needed to spend? Perhaps. But the economy was rolling, the firm was a privately held partnership, and the partners knew in their guts that it was money well spent.

And it wasn't just any old kind of training that was being offered, either. A visitor strolling by the offices and cubicles of the training professionals in St. Charles and Chicago would see scores of plaques, certificates and statues on display—all evidence of award-winning training courses designed and delivered by

Accenture for both classroom instruction and electronic learning. Consistent with its culture of innovation, Accenture professionals had pioneered the applications of many training techniques now accepted as standard in the corporate world, such as goal-based learning. Simulation-based learning—thrusting learners into role-playing in simulated real-life conditions to reinforce lessons and shape desired behaviors—was advanced by Accenture and became part of most classroom experiences.

As simulation moved into the electronic realm—called "business simulation" at first and then "performance simulation"—Accenture was also out in front. An early performance simulator developed in 1994 to improve the risk management capabilities of employees of GE Capital (now called GE Consumer Finance) delivered huge benefits for that company and was vivid proof of the effectiveness of simulation as a learning experience. Students with no financial background at all who had gone through this training were outscoring CPAs on some control examinations.

Accenture had its fair share of visionaries, as well, and knew how to give these people the funding and leeway to keep Accenture out in front. In the early 1990s, Accenture had pioneered a concept called "integrated performance support"—a version of the electronic performance support systems that were beginning to augment stand-alone computer-based training (CBT) courses. The vision—to package integrated resource information, tools, job aids and training at a single desktop to support just-in-time performance needs of workers—was so far ahead of its time that only now are the technologies in place to support it and create realistic, cost-effective solutions.

And at the heart of it all remained the central training facility in St. Charles. Almost single-handedly keeping local limousine services in business—shuttling students morning and night to and from Chicago's O'Hare airport—the St. Charles campus was home to about 1,000 students each week during its busiest years in 1998 and 1999. The St. Charles experience was a vital part of the culture of Accenture, bringing together workers from North and South America, Asia, Africa, Europe and Australia—in the classroom, at the lunch and dinner tables, and (perhaps most enjoyably of all) at the social center when the day's work was over and a few precious hours could be spared for relaxation. Overnight accommodations were somewhat spartan, perhaps—a single bed, a desk and a bathroom—but with little time to sleep, it hardly mattered.

Although client work has always taken precedence over most other responsibilities at Accenture, employees and partners alike were expected to work around their client duties and to be there in St. Charles, as scheduled, when the time came either to attend or teach a class. The opportunity to be taught by successful and experienced senior partners at Accenture was one of the big draws of the entire training program. And a related initiative, called "Partners Are in Residence," or "PAIR," brought executives to St. Charles not necessarily to teach, but to mingle with students, eat meals with them and generally provide informal mentoring.

So there it is: as the twentieth century comes to a close, Accenture is growing at 20 percent annually and the Internet explosion is fueling a frenzy for advanced technology and implementation skills. By the mid-1990s Accenture has more work—and more work in the pipeline—than it can actually handle with its current workforce, and recruiters and trainers alike are busy finding the best people around and equipping them with the knowledge and skills needed for their growth, and the growth of the firm.

So what could possibly go wrong?

Turmoil and change

Fast-forward now to the year 2001. It's a gray November morning, and the first signs of an approaching Chicago winter are in the air. The two bronze statues still carry on their eternal conversation in the courtyard of the St. Charles training facility. The problem is, they are about the only human figures to be found anywhere on campus.

The training facility's empty halls in late 2001 were not the result of failed training investments, of course. They were the result of the crisis facing global businesses—and US businesses in particular—following the terrorist attacks on New York City and Washington, D.C., on September 11, 2001. With a temporary freeze on business travel, the central training facility used by Accenture was, for all intents and purposes, shuttered.

However, the darkened classrooms were also, in a sense, symbolic of the dark times that had fallen on the proud training organization of Accenture. It had been a tumultuous time for Accenture, to say the least, and the effects on the company's training programs had been felt long before terrorists flew airplanes into the World Trade Center and the Pentagon.

The first event was something that hit the entire economy, though consulting organizations worse than many others: the bursting of the Internet bubble in the early years of the new century, and the end of a period of almost unprecedented technology spending and investment. For the first time in its history, Accenture's revenues stagnated. The $700 million annual training investment, previously untouchable, was now under scrutiny.

The Accenture culture was being affected by layoffs as well. Accenture has always been fiercely meritocratic. Its "up or out" advancement policy for its client-facing workforce meant that few workers were ever total strangers to the possibility of being asked to leave. But, in fact, Accenture always had been able to find a place for bright people, recognizing the long-term value of thought leaders within its workforce, even if those employees were not directly bringing in as high a percentage of client revenues as others. In the difficult economy of 2001 and 2002, however, layoffs were hitting the training organization particularly hard.

Finally, as if anything more was needed to stress the company's culture, this was also the time when Accenture was being reorganized, with a new name (the company was formerly known as Andersen Consulting) and a new existence as a publicly held company. It was a challenging time, requiring a great deal of leadership energy. With an initial share offering in July 2001, Accenture and its people faced a new challenge: dealing with the quarterly expectations of investors and analysts, and a new mindset that required taking both a long-term and a short-term, or quarterly, focus.

Yet the challenge facing Accenture and its training organization at that point was caused not only by new business models and external markets. The manner in which events transpired brings to mind a character in Ernest Hemingway's novel *The Sun Also Rises* who, when asked how he went bankrupt, replies, "First gradually, and then suddenly." The freeze on airline trips following the 9/11 disaster had been merely the immediate crisis that had brought to a head the more gradual organizational changes, leadership decisions and budget reallocations that had made the training organization and its programs leaner than it could stand. The declining employee satisfaction scores Accenture was now experiencing were not the result of legal issues or public offerings. They were caused by an organization struggling to keep faith with its promises to its people to provide world-class learning and development opportunities.

It actually was these other organizational factors, and the disparity between Accenture's claims and the reality when it came to learning and development, that were on the mind of Accenture's executive in charge of training, Don Vanthournout, as he walked the darkened halls in St. Charles in November of 2001.

Diagnosis

Vanthournout is what is referred to as a "lifer" at Accenture. Having joined the organization as a recruit right out of college, he has been with Accenture more than 20 years. He worked in the financial services operating group, first as a "line" consultant (as in, the "front lines" of client work) and then with the HR organization. He took the helm of the training organization in 2000, assuming the official title of chief learning officer in 2005.

Because Vanthournout himself had benefited from what was called "mainline training"—the shared core of common training courses that churned out the well-prepared new consultants of the 1980s—he well understood both how and why the training situation had changed so dramatically over the past several years. His first move as the year 2002 began was to meet with as many of Accenture's partners as possible—one at a time or a few at a time—to help them understand where things stood and to get their ownership and buy-in to what needed to be done to remedy the situation.

He made a shrewd move: he showed each partner a chart of the mainline training courses that each of those partners had been through themselves as younger professionals, and asked them if this was still how they understood the Accenture training curriculum. When they answered affirmatively, he opened the chart up to its full size to show them the reality: from a shared core of more than a dozen courses offered to employees in the 1980s and 1990s, the core had shrunk to two courses: an introductory course for analysts (the term given to new employees) and a seminar for newly promoted executives. "They were shocked," recalls Vanthournout.

It was that disconnect between perception and reality when it came to training and development that was causing some disillusionment among many of Accenture's newer hires. Accenture's recruiting success through the years has been built on the heavy involvement of the partners themselves, who often return to their alma maters to speak to college students, share their own experiences and sell Accenture as a great place to work. The training opportunities at Accenture were a big part of that sell job. In fact, a survey of college graduates conducted in 2000 had underscored Accenture's advantage in this area: survey respondents indicated they actually would be willing to work for Accenture for less annual salary based solely on the strength of the training program. That is, they were willing to take less now for the prospect of making more later.

But when that recruit became an employee in 2000 or 2001, the promised training curriculum never materialized. And the disillusionment showed up immediately in employee satisfaction scores.

What had happened? It turned out to be a valuable lesson in the unintended consequences of organizational change—changes in operating structures and business models. As Vanthournout puts it, "No one ever set out to kill the core training curriculum.

But through a series of tactical decisions, shared training had gone away."

By 2000, Accenture was still in the process of reinventing itself as a company that did more than systems installation work. Not "systems integration," but "business integration" had become its strategic catch phrase throughout the 1990s, and Accenture had reorganized itself around the four areas it believed to be critical to that work: strategy, process, technology and people (called "change management"). To each of the four leaders of these groups, the old common training curriculum seemed passé: change management professionals needed change management training; strategy people needed strategy. The implication was that different parts of the workforce would now receive different kinds of training based on their roles and responsibilities.

"Empowering these four different groups to design and deliver their own training content seemed a good idea at the time," says Vanthournout. "But a consequence was that the common curriculum—on which Accenture had once built a shared sense of culture and purpose—had eroded over time."

Large-scale business changes also were affecting the training curriculum, changes that altered Accenture's understanding of the mission-critical workforces—the right people with the right skills—necessary to face future business needs. Several key areas in the traditional technology consulting world already were undergoing commoditization at the turn of the century. Off-the-shelf software and the rise of technology standards were altering the systems integration playing field, and Accenture's corporate leaders were laying the groundwork to augment the company's traditional high-value consulting work with transformational outsourcing and affiliated businesses in areas like HR, learning and customer service.

Helping to lead the charge in the learning and HR areas was Vanthournout's boss, Jill Smart, Accenture's senior managing director for human resources. "Both short-term and long-term economics were affecting our industry," says Smart. "In the short term, we were coping with necessary budget cuts. In the long term, however, we were undergoing a fairly dramatic workforce reorganization to respond to strategic imperatives in the market-place. We were moving from a pure consulting organization, one with a fairly large homogeneous workforce, to a consulting and outsourcing company with several different kinds of workforces depending on how the work was to be sourced."

Accenture's challenge wasn't as simple as "going back to ba-sics." As Smart notes, "Although all of us felt the tug to go back to a unifying core curriculum, the fact is that we weren't the same firm and the marketplace wasn't the same as it was in the 1980s. The people we had to train were now much more diverse and the company was more global. The needs of our clients were different. We had a significant journey in front of us, but first we had to figure out what kind of journey it was."

The business journey ahead

The transformation and reinvention of the learning culture at Accenture was not going to happen overnight, and it would not be accomplished by throwing money at the problem. One thing was certain: Accenture was not going to be spending $700 million a year on training anymore.

Early on, Vanthournout and the team he assembled made a decision to frame the entire journey not in training terms, but in business terms. No one at Accenture was about to give back any of the training awards they had received over the years, but Vanthournout knew that the very richness of the training experi-ences Accenture was designing was in fact symptomatic of a deeper disconnect between training and the needs of the business.

"The mindset of the central training group at Accenture," says Vanthournout, "had been mostly about doing new and different and better training than had ever been done before. So it was spending lots of money building very expensive training vehicles that were breakthrough courses: engaging classroom experiences, rich multimedia content, state-of-the art CBT and online training. But on balance it had become more important to get the delivery right than to get the content right. And measuring the impact on business performance hadn't happened much at all. The training group measured satisfaction of the learners at the end of the class, but 'satisfaction' doesn't really tell you whether or not the learners are going to be more effective at their jobs than they had been before."

So the team Vanthournout assembled to lead the journey ahead was designed to be a business team more than anything. Accenture was aiming very high with it goals: to bring consistency back to the way training was planned, designed and implemented; to increase the business impact of learning at Accenture; and to do that while improving operational efficiency. They were going to leverage the very best that the training industry had to offer—especially the newer e-learning and knowledge management technologies that were dramatically lowering the cost to serve while in many cases also dramatically improving the impact of the training experience on performance. With budgets drastically reduced, doing more with less would be a prerequisite.

Accenture was now going to be "running the learning organization as a business," as the group came to articulate it. The benefits: better leverage of technology, better vendor management, a healthy dose of outsourcing to actually design the learning in a way that would be both more efficient and more effective. And, perhaps the most important benefit would be a better articulated curriculum: a return to the shared learning experiences and the re-birth of the St. Charles training facility, to re-invigorate the distinctive learning culture at Accenture. At the same time, the focus would be on more targeted training delivered to employees when it was truly needed: "just-in-time" learning, not "just-in-case" learning.

The focus would also be on meeting the needs of the business—the client-facing operating groups and service lines at Accenture, as well as the company's different workforces. But no longer would training proceed by ceding responsibility to the client groups and hoping for the best. The client groups and the training organizations would now share responsibility for enabling Accenture's people with the right knowledge and training.

Human and organizational value:
The final business frontier

Because the learning transformation journey at Accenture was framed in business terms by Vanthournout and his team, the story of the journey is a business story: about how one company—Accenture—advanced toward high performance through learning, knowledge management and the transformation of its workforce. By extension, however, it is about how other organizations can do the same.

The transformation of an organization's workforce for business advantage is one of the last great unexplored frontiers in management thinking today. Much has been written and said about leveraging workforce capabilities more effectively, but very little has been executed to full advantage. The difficulty in fully capitalizing on an organization's human resources—its human value, intellectual value and social value—to achieve high performance is often masked because of the fog of words that organizations create around their people. Many annual reports dutifully note that the company's people are the basis of its competitive advantage, but relatively few executives know how to plan and execute a workforce transformation initiative with the rigor necessary to produce measurable results.

The use of information technology and business process transformation for business advantage are well-worn paths. Many executives still see their roles revolving around grander business strategy, while matters of "human resources" are left to the operational attentions of lower-level managers. Gradually, however, the research is starting to show that it is not the strategy, process and technology levers alone but the human performance levers which, thrown properly and in the right combination, produce the biggest impact on business results. Senior-level executives are beginning to speak more often about issues like "employee engagement": how can they best tap into the collective intelligence of their people and engage them in their work, for their benefit and the benefit of the entire enterprise? University researchers such as

Gary Becker, Jeffrey Pfeffer, Mark Huselid and others are casting the hard light of metrics on a host of workforce-related business influences. In his book *Human Equation,* Pfeffer quotes from a variety of studies that find far less correlation between various high-level business strategies and business performance than among many "humbler" kinds of HR practices such as profit sharing and results-oriented employee performance appraisals.

Accenture, too, has made a significant contribution to measuring the value of human resources and human capital with its learning ROI research, detailed in Chapter 3. That ROI study was just one of several things that Accenture got right as it reinvigorated its culture of learning. Indeed, this book is organized around those factors: creating a vision and sustaining a program through rigorous adherence to that vision; linking human capital investments to business benefits; putting in place the governance and leadership structures that increase a program's chances of success; ensuring that the actual classroom and electronic training developed creates what the team came to call "phenomenal" learning experiences; and maximizing the operational efficiency of learning.

We invite you to come along with us on this story of Accenture's transformation because we believe these experiences can help any organization achieve high performance through a "return on learning."

- This is the story about how one company advanced toward high performance through learning, knowledge management and the transformation of its workforce—and, by extension, how other organizations can do the same.
- High-quality learning and training do not necessarily translate into business results. Enterprise learning must be driven with the end in mind: the business results to be achieved.
- From a business-centric perspective, learning can get out of alignment with business need. Executives can become too far removed from the core learning engine of the company, and they need to increase their understanding and involvement in how their workforce is being enabled and leveraged for high performance.
- Effective learning can drive high performance in any industry: better ways to create and market new products and services, to increase customer satisfaction and retention, to attract and retain the best workers, and to use technology, information systems and networks to improve operating efficiency, to innovate and to succeed in the long term.

Two

A Vision for Learning and Business Impact

If a company manufactures a product, and has $700 million a year invested in its manufacturing plant, its executives will make sure that equipment is operating at peak efficiency and capacity every hour of the day. The company's very existence depends upon how effectively it can transform raw materials into products of value in the marketplace.

The existence and long-term success of a company like Accenture, however, depends on the solutions and assets it creates for clients—in other words, on effectively and efficiently transforming raw knowledge into business value. As Jill Smart puts it, "What Accenture sells are assets and knowledge—business value delivered through people. It could be new knowledge capital created for a particular client, or capital we've created elsewhere but leveraged in many places. In either case, our value is derived from what's in our people's heads. Our people represent our R&D and our product development, all at the same time. So what we were looking to do, ultimately, as we started our journey to reinvent learning and training at Accenture, was to instill in our executives what I once heard a successful manufacturing executive say about R&D at his company: 'We don't cut the R&D budget here, even in the leanest of economic conditions. Because it's our essential DNA; it's what makes us distinctive.'"

In fact, Accenture's recent research into the characteristics of high performance confirmed that learning is an essential part of the "performance anatomy" of an organization. Along with market focus and distinctive capabilities, learning is one of the building blocks of high performance. Creating optimal performance anatomy requires developing people who enable high-performance businesses to achieve extraordinary levels of employee productivity. In this way, high performers create a "talent multiplier"—achieving superior business results versus their peers per dollar of investment in their workforces.

Don Vanthournout had been charged with restoring the learning function to its preeminent position at Accenture, in order to improve the performance anatomy of the company and to help Accenture advance toward high performance. Vanthournout recalls, as he set out to speak with the company's leadership, how one executive articulated the challenge to him. "The chief executive of one of our operating groups told me early on that my challenge was to make learning one of the top three issues that our executive group, especially the CEO, is working on, because the leadership team can't worry about everything. If a certain topic or domain is not on the short list of issues, it's very difficult to get executive attention and buy in."

Vanthournout formulated a strategy for engaging Accenture's leadership at more than an intellectual level about what had happened to the culture of learning at the company, and what the consequences and risks were if the existing situation continued. When Vanthournout met with many of the company's partners in early 2002, he showed these executives that many of their presumptions about the current state of learning and training at their own company were no longer true. Short-term needs and goals had been allowed to interfere with the longer-term development of the people, and Accenture's distinctive edge in the marketplace could be weakened if something were not done.

Vanthournout had the numbers to make his case. Per-person investments in learning and training had been cut almost in half over the previous couple of years. Reducing the budget alone is not itself a problem, of course, as long as the money is being spent wisely and for maximum effect. But other numbers showed that the leadership's commitment to employee learning had weakened. One troubling statistic showed that more than 40 percent of requests for classroom training the previous year at Accenture had either been immediately denied, or the employee had been forced to cancel because of other work commitments.

The state of the company's commitment to learning had become reminiscent of the old story of the man who could never fix his leaky roof: when it was raining, he couldn't go up on the roof; when it was sunny, the roof wasn't leaking. In this case, when business was up, executives did not feel they could spare people from client work to go to learning events; when business was down, executives didn't want to spend scarce financial resources on a non-revenue-generating function like learning. Vanthournout recalls, "We had to change the culture back to the point where training and learning were top priorities to everyone, at every level of the organization. There are lots of priorities, of course. Having your employees chargeable at clients is obviously a priority, too, but we had to move leadership back to the point where learning and training were not just 'nice to have' things when there's nothing else to do. We had to get their buy-in to the belief that learning is a strategic investment—a priority in good economic times and in bad. Of course, there's some flexibility to alter budgets and shift things around to meet urgent needs, but you don't take your learning investment to zero when times get tough."

Vanthournout also had the numbers to show how the wavering commitment to employee learning and training was affecting the workforce. He put the matter in fairly stark terms: "The deal we have made with our people," he said, "has been broken."

Employee surveys showed that, throughout Accenture, although 82 percent of employees said that increasing the commitment to ongoing learning would increase their job satisfaction, only just more than 50 percent said they had a favorable impression of the learning and training function. Only about one-third reported receiving direction from their superiors about ongoing development. Too few said that the training they had planned or requested had been approved. Others wondered if attending training might actually be bad for their careers; if taking time away from client work to attend a class reduced their chargeability numbers compared with peers, did training actually increase their risk of being laid off? Another part of the task ahead, therefore, was to gain the trust back from the workforce: to reengage people in training and to make learning a positive career driver for employees once again.

Diminished execution of stewardship responsibilities was partly behind the decline. Participation by the partners in Accenture classrooms had gone down precipitously: from 69 taking part in courses in 2001 to only 11 in 2002. The "Partners Are in Residence" program at the main training facility in St. Charles (a program created to increase the interaction of newer employees with more experienced executives) had dwindled from 102 partners in 2000 to 61 in 2001. In 2002, the program was on pace to put only about two dozen leadership partners in St. Charles.

But Vanthournout had the upside numbers, too, the carrot as well as the stick: the news about the value that could be created through a renewed commitment to the learning culture of Accenture. In the first phase of what became a groundbreaking study of the return on training investment, Vanthournout's team had analyzed research data from a number of sources. A survey of more than 2,300 recent hires at Accenture revealed, for example, that the opportunity for training and development was the number-one reason they had come to work for Accenture. And it was an external study from 2001 that had showed recruits actually would be willing to work for Accenture for a lower annual salary than they would accept for competing companies, simply on the basis of the perceived excellence of the Accenture training program.

Training and learning also were key elements in retaining the company's best employees. Analysis of more than 30,000 responses to Accenture's annual Global People Survey showed that employees who said they had access to the training they needed to be successful were more likely to think they were being compensated fairly, twice as likely to expect to be with the company in two years and more than six times more likely to think of Accenture as a "great place to work."

The document Vanthournout used in his discussions with the partners was dated March 2002. His final report to Accenture leadership—detailing a vision for learning and the plan to realize that vision—was due in October. The diagnosis phase of the renewal and reinvention of learning at Accenture was now just about over. The months ahead would be challenging indeed.

Choosing the team

Jill Smart was an ideal person to oversee the journey that lay ahead for Accenture and its learning organization. A veteran of more than 20 years with Accenture, leading large-scale technology projects, Smart's leadership style invests a great deal of authority in the people on her team, and she knows how to find the right people to implement large-scale change programs. She had to make some difficult personnel moves at first to put the right leadership in place in the learning organization, called the "capability development group," but she was convinced that the journey ahead was a business journey, not just a training one, and that it would take fresh leadership to see the challenge the right way.

By bringing in Vanthournout to head the group—where his title eventually became chief learning officer—Smart believed she already had the right leader for this complex program. "Don has many strengths," Smart recalls, "including the ability to build loyalty in his teams and to get a lot out of them. But beyond that, Don has the ability to deal with ambiguity better than many of us who seem to live in a more binary world, and who tend to build success on a more black-and-white view of reality. The situation we faced truly was gray and ambiguous. So it really helped us to have two leadership styles here. Not 'good cop/bad cop' but maybe 'intangible/tangible.' When you're changing a business, you're changing the people and the culture. It's not totally fuzzy—it's not quite as ambiguous as art or music; but a culture isn't a machine or an information system, either. You can't always say, as you can with more precision when designing a financial system, 'This module will be ready in three weeks.' So you need balance, and I knew right away that we had achieved that."

For his part, Vanthournout assembled a team which, he notes, was more of a business team focused on corporate education than it was an education team trying to have a business impact. In charge of curriculum planning and development was Kurt Olson, with 20 years of experience at Accenture, most spent in technology and systems delivery, where he gained experience managing large, complex systems projects. Brad Kolar, another long-term Accenture veteran (who later became chief learning officer for the University of Chicago Hospitals), would work from an overall strategy point of view, putting together the vision and the plan to carry the training organization through its work in the months and years ahead.

Andy White, in charge of training operations, especially classroom operations at the St. Charles facility, had been with the training organization the longest. Prior to his training responsibilities, White had worked for almost a decade doing client work as part of the consulting organization. John Ceisel, Tom Barfield and Samir Desai had worked with Vanthournout in his earlier role as head of the organization which develops the methodologies, productivity tools and training for Accenture. Ceisel, another team member with more than 20 years of experience with Accenture, had worked with both technology and learning; he had been a training solution planner, working with different groups from around the company to identify and deliver their training needs. Barfield had been a member of the product distribution and support organization, and Desai was part of the training development and delivery organization focused on leveraging technology to deliver training solutions. All three of them were part of a sub-team that delivered advanced technologies to make the strategy come alive. Tad Waddington also joined the team as director of performance measurement. In addition to his years of experience with Accenture, Waddington had been a research director with the Gallup Organization and has a

Ph.D. in measurement, evaluation and statistical analysis from the University of Chicago. Waddington's role would become crucial in making the business case for reinventing training and learning at Accenture, and for gaining the vital external validation—including academic validation—for what Vanthournout's entire team had set out to accomplish.

In effect, Vanthournout asked these team members to take a risk with him: to put their professional backgrounds on the line to see if, together, they could successfully reverse the situation at Accenture and reestablish the company as a provider of world-class learning opportunities for its people—great learning experiences that also produced great business results.

After a series of initial meetings, this core team created a new mission statement for itself: to "create the premier professional education program, building leaders and a differentiated workforce, which enables the acceleration of Accenture's strategy." Underpinning this mission, however, were several important principles that would guide the team in creating a vision for the reinvention of learning at Accenture. In this vision, professional education at Accenture would:

- Become a strategic investment of the highest priority, even during difficult economic times.
- Be measured according to how well it supported the business strategy and improved the performance of the company overall.
- Differentiate Accenture from its competitors, both in its form (high-quality and innovative training vehicles) and in its results (the improvement in performance resulting from the training).
- Offer exceptional development opportunities that stretch and challenge individuals and teams.
- Be delivered with world-class efficiency, maximizing the value of every dollar spent.
- Recapture the value of the central global training facility in St. Charles, Illinois, as the home and heart of learning

for the company, strengthening individuals and the entire company culture.

- Involve leaders teaching leaders.
- Build the Accenture brand of people—individuals who can lead and create value in any context.

A vision in alignment with the company's core values

One of the things that Vanthournout and his team got right over the next few years was an effective mode of governance and leadership for the learning reinvention program—one that also achieved buy-in and cooperation from the very highest leadership echelons at Accenture. (This part of the story is covered in Chapter 4.)

Andy White recalls, "From our very first meeting, we were already talking about how we could create a vision for learning that really energized the leadership of the company. Don had already made a compelling case with our executives that the status quo of global learning was no longer in alignment with the way they had been trained themselves. The old 'Accenture way' of doing things that had been engrained in them through the core curriculum and the St. Charles experience was no longer in place. They resonated with the problem; now we needed them to resonate with the solution."

The approach the team took was to tie the vision to the core values of the company: stewardship, best people, client value creation, respect for the individual, integrity and one global network. White says, "By tying our work to the core values of Accenture, we simply said to our leadership, 'Here is what you have said matters to Accenture; here is what you have already told us you want to build our success on. These are *your* excellent ideas. Now, here are the implications for what you have said you want to accomplish when it comes to revitalizing our learning culture.'"

Accenture also had in place a leadership model, and Vanthournout and his team decided to focus the execution of the vision of the new learning organization around the three components of that model: *value creators* for the company and its clients, *people developers* on behalf of the workforce and *business operators* who could be effective stewards of company resources. Says White, "Anchoring our vision and plans to our corporate values and to our own leadership model was a key success factor. It gave us a structure; it based our work around what we valued most, and then traced that all the way down to the details of what those values meant for how we led our people. What do those value statements mean to our newest hires? To our senior managers? To our different kinds of workforces serving different industries? Our leadership resonated very deeply with that plan."

Value creator

First of all, the team declared, training and learning were to be planned and executed according to the business value produced for the company. To make that happen would require pursuing a rigorous program to measure the impact of Accenture's learning programs, and to determine the company's overall return on investment—the "return on learning." Value creation also meant that the learning offerings would be planned and executed according to the most important business needs and strategies of the company. "For years," says Vanthournout, "many courses within our overall learning curriculum were developed based on who yelled the loudest or who had the most clout." Instead, Vanthournout and team determined at the outset that the enablement strategy of the company would be continuously tied directly to the critical elements of Accenture's strategy and business model. "We said, 'Instead, from now on, the development of our learning offerings is going to be based on what we need from our people to deliver our business strategy.' This changed the game and took the advantage away from the person with the loudest voice or the budget of the day, and gave it instead to those with a clear sense of how we could more strategically invest in training and building our people."

The team also incorporated into its vision a means of explicitly linking results from learning to both internal and external stakeholders. As shown in Figure 1, six success factors for the learning strategy were especially critical to maximizing the return on investment in learning—not only for Accenture's leadership, but also for Accenture's external stakeholders. It was vital to create learning opportunities that made Accenture an attractive place for top-notch employees to stay and grow, and a place where recruits would want to come to work.

The area of "value creation and delivery," in particular, represented a significant shift for Accenture's learning organization. As Smart puts it, "If we were going to successfully run learning as a business, we realized that we would need to think in strategic business terms. So, instead of just focusing on resolving knowledge and skills gaps, for example, we needed to focus on resolving performance issues that can impede business results. Instead of just focusing on the delivery of learning, we needed our primary focus to be on how we could best grow individuals who can deliver on our business strategy—who can become masters in creating value for our clients. That would, in turn, lead our clients to want to partner with us because they would know they could rely on superior people with superior knowledge."

Figure 1. Planning the impact of training on internal and external stakeholders

Added up, all of this meant altering the traditional focus of Accenture's learning organization, which in most cases had been on programs with large audiences, and instead prioritizing training investments based on how to create a workforce that creates the most value for the organization. Says Vanthournout, "This shift was saying, in effect, we still want to build specific skills in people but, even more important, we want to build the right kind of people who can deliver our business strategy."

People developer

Every training or learning department has, as its most explicit charge, the development of the organization's people. But "development" meaning what, exactly? Like most companies, Accenture previously had framed the development discussion in terms of specific roles and skills: given the relevant work environment and the client's needs, someone at "X" level, with "Y" background, needed "Z" set of skills. With the new approach, learning investments at Accenture would focus first on the common set of behaviors, skills and capabilities needed to succeed personally, and on behalf of the entire company, regardless of the specific role or context in which a person was placed. By taking a role-specific orientation, a person never really can achieve full competence, especially in the field of technology, because the field is constantly changing and new skills are always required. But from a business viewpoint, the team could identify a set of common characteristics of what could be called the "Accenture professional." These included the capability to:

- Understand how a business creates value, and then use that understanding to drive client value.
- Develop and articulate a compelling point of view, and mobilize others to take action on that point of view.
- Embody the Accenture culture and brand; act with purpose, based on the company's core values; and set a standard for professional excellence.

- Provide innovative solutions to business problems and innovation in solving those problems.
- Understand and be able to leverage the tools and resources available to maximize value delivery.

Armed with this new way of looking at training and learning, the team could then begin plotting the development of the learning strategy for such a professional. As Vanthournout notes, "As a services organization, our people—and the assets and solutions they help to create—are our products. So what we were doing was, in reality, defining our largest product offerings."

At the same time, as noted earlier, this emphasis on developing common attributes in an Accenture professional had to be balanced by the fact that the workforce served by the training organization was no longer the monolithic one of the 1980s and 1990s. In fact, Accenture's identity as a consulting, technology and outsourcing company meant that it now was serving clients through the work of four distinct workforces, each with a different set of needed skills and a different cost base:

- The Consulting workforce. Employees with deep specialist knowledge in business, technical and functional areas, and involved in business consulting, process design work and the application of technology to business.
- The Services workforce. Employees assigned to long-term outsourcing engagements with clients, for whom Accenture manages and provides increasingly specialized business operations, such as finance and accounting, IT, applications development and maintenance, help desk services and HR.
- The Solutions workforce. Employees who serve as technology specialists, working with Accenture's global network of consulting and services experts to develop, implement and maintain leading-edge technologies for Accenture clients.

- The Enterprise workforce. Employees within a dedicated corporate functions workforce who run Accenture's business, while providing a wide range of services to support Accenture's client teams, outsourcing units and other businesses.

Finding the learning strategy that could reach and maintain this balance between common professional attributes and unique workforce requirements was a challenge, to be sure. Andy White recalls, "Executives with any organization always ask for deeper skills in their people. The problem is, how are you going to get people who have the time to take classes and learn all those deeper skills? Because training alone isn't the answer. Professional development requires not only training but also extensive and varied experiences, connecting with others, living the life of a professional, collaborating with colleagues, interacting with clients. How do you take people who come into our organization—many of them from very technical backgrounds in computer science or engineering—and turn them into industry subsegment experts or experts in key business processes like supply chain or CRM? How do you create someone who will grow up some day to be a visionary for the financial services industry or the field of electronics and high-tech? A person who feels comfortable going in and having a conversation with the CEO of a Fortune 100 company? That's pretty hard to do."

The approach was to return to the traditional Accenture core curriculum strategy while augmenting it with the specific skills necessary for the type of workforce and/or type of industry in which an employee works. So the core learning programs would be put back in place as a way to develop the Accenture professional: core skills linked to the company's business strategy; reinforcement of culture and values; and building critical professional skills such as leadership, relationship building, program and project management, and selling. Moving out from the core, additional categories of skills would deal with the particular needs of an employee working in a specialized industry or domain environment:

- Deep functional competence, specialty and delivery excellence skills
- Deep industry skills
- Job readiness skills to prepare people for a specific role or task
- Deep understanding of how to implement Accenture's business strategy

More work remained, of course, to define these skills in terms meaningful to each of the workforces and industry groups within Accenture. But this was a solid beginning.

Business operator

The final component upon which Vanthournout and his team based their reinvention vision was on running the learning organization not as a privileged entity with a sacrosanct budget, nor as a mere cost center, but as a business—with an explicit role to play in delivering business results and responsibility for improving the overall cost-effectiveness of its operations.

Developing this business orientation would prove to be one of the biggest changes in values for the internal capability development group, and those with a more traditional approach to internal training. Accenture's learning organization in the 1980s and 1990s had been driven more by delivering award-winning training than by delivering that training on time and on budget. Now, with a focus on effective business operations as a core value, Vanthournout's team was committing to the same rigor as their counterparts working with clients: they would deliver what they had promised, on the dates to which they had committed, within the agreed budget.

Creating that operational rigor involved retooling the processes by which training assets were defined, planned and built. The new training organization at Accenture needed to develop delivery and program management credibility with senior leadership.

This led to a dramatic shift in how work was tracked. Members of Vanthournout's leadership team were empowered to deliver, but they also knew that they were going to be held accountable for the results.

As each piece of the overall plan was delivered on time while meeting the necessary business requirements, leadership's confidence in Vanthournout and his team grew. This allowed the training organization to take on even greater challenges. Accenture's leadership team came to know that money invested within the training organization was going to be wisely spent, and that it would deliver high-impact results. For the most recent fiscal year, to take one example, Vanthournout and his team delivered all of the projects requested of them with an overall (positive) budget variance of less than .05 percent.

Planning, tracking and communicating results

To achieve that kind of delivery rigor, the evaluation team—led by Bruce Aaron, another member of the capability development group—adopted a tool from Accenture's core systems building methodology to create a unique and innovative Accenture asset, the Accenture V-Model of Learning and Training (see Figure 2). This model was put in place to link business needs to the specific learning assets to be developed to meet those needs, and then to measure the impact of the asset on workforce capability and on the performance of the business. The V-model bridges local business context, best practices in evaluation, and the shift in emphasis from traditional training activity to self-directed learning, knowledge management and performance improvement approaches.

The model begins at top left with the original business need—a challenge or opportunity phrased in business terms. It proceeds through solution design and delivery and ends with the determination of the return on investment for the learning solution—the "return on learning." The left side of the model

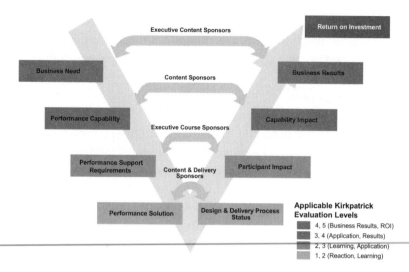

Figure 2. *The Accenture V-Model of Learning and Training*

comprises analysis, design, development and delivery tasks. It proceeds from macro-level analysis activities (starting with the business need and definition of business requirements) through finer detail specifications (such as functional requirements) and specific design decisions. In these stages of learning development, the business need is translated into human performance requirements and solution designs.

The right side of the model focuses on measurement and evaluation. Each activity there defines a specific set of measurements for the corresponding analysis, design, and development activities on the left side of the model. The scope of the measured impact broadens at the top of the model, with measurements focused on overall business results and ROI, when those results are compared to the cost of the solution.

One key to the effectiveness of the V-model is its symmetry. On the left side, representing analysis of learning needs and the design of solutions, the model requires that a development team also develop the metrics that will link the plans with the results. This ensures tight linkages between the analysis/design phase and the measurement phase. When used properly to guide the development of training and learning solutions, the V-model results in solutions linked to business needs and metrics that are tied to performance objectives.

The model also ensures that sponsors and decision makers (see the middle of the "V") get the metrics and results that are most meaningful to them, given their roles. Those who serve as sponsors for a particular learning offering will be most interested in metrics that indicate how successfully that course was administered and the impact it had on participants. Those who ask for particular content to be reflected in a set of courses (because of marketplace need in serving clients or customers) want to see the impact of the learning experience on workforce capabilities. Executive leadership wants to see the business results coming out of the overall learning environment.

Says Vanthournout, "What the V-model gave us was a way to plan and implement our learning programs, and then also communicate their value. Most important, it was an approach that did not start by assuming that training was the best solution and then work backward to business need. Frankly, a formal training solution should never be the automatic response to a workforce performance need or business need. Training can be an expensive response, so it should be reserved for situations where it's critical or truly appropriate. Maybe the response instead should be something to increase motivation; or maybe knowledge sharing is the answer, or a mentoring program. The key is to focus first on what the performance needs are in the workforce and then determine the appropriate responses, mapped to measurable results, that the company should take, given budget and resource constraints."

Those constraints were very real now for Accenture. The budget for the training and learning programs at Accenture was going to be one-third to one-half less than it had been in the late-90s period, and the number of learning professionals on the core team was also going to be significantly reduced. Yet Vanthournout's team had set the aggressive goal to actually increase the impact and effectiveness of learning.

So the team's initial work with the V-model of learning now led them to a real "stretch" bit of work: how would they begin to describe the very top right side of the V-model, where business impact was measured? What *was* the return on investment in learning for Accenture? What was its impact on the company's bottom line? Answers to those questions would be vital not just for academic reasons, but for the very practical reason of ensuring maximum buy-in to the learning transformation program from the most senior levels of Accenture.

- For companies in the knowledge business, achieving high performance depends on how effectively and efficiently they can turn raw knowledge into business value for clients or customers. Their people represent their R&D and their product development, all at the same time.
- Successfully transforming learning to deliver business results depends on getting the buy-in from the top echelon of leadership in the organization. Learning needs to be a priority in both good economic times and challenging times—maybe most especially in the latter case.
- Learning and training opportunities can be a differentiator in attracting and retaining employees.
- Creating a learning function that has an impact on the business means creating a learning team with strong business skills.
- An enterprise should build a learning strategy founded on the core values of the organization, as well as its primary leadership values.
- Many organizations create learning programs based on transitory business headlines or on who shouts the loudest. Instead, learning must be continuously tied directly to current business goals and on the critical elements of the strategy and business model.
- Rather than just focusing on the development and delivery of learning in the most efficient way possible, companies must focus how to grow the kinds of individuals who can deliver on business strategy.

Three

Proving the ROI in Learning

"Your goal," one of the senior leaders at Accenture had said to Don Vanthournout after being briefed on the vision for reinventing learning at the company, "is to convince the top executive team that reinvigorating learning needs to be one of the top three priorities of the company." That is easier said than done, even at a company like Accenture with a long heritage of advanced thinking about human performance and learning, and the importance of training to achieving high performance.

Why? In part because of the enormous pressures and constant barrage of burning issues facing any leadership team. It's difficult to fathom what a typical day is like for those who run today's major companies: the daily calendar scheduled down to six-minute increments, meetings planned during car rides to airports so as not to waste any time, the press of analysts and other stakeholders, the constant clamor of different internal groups for investment dollars. Those sympathetic to the importance of human performance issues may find it difficult to understand why their topic would not naturally be top of mind for any CEO. Remember, though, that any particular business function or need takes its place amid a chorus of others and the competing voices of those who think that the supply chain, or procurement, or outsourcing, or selling to the small and medium business segment—and on and on—should also be one of the top three issues. And, in the end, being an executive does not come with an extra ten hours to the day.

There is a second reason, though, why workforce performance

investments often are not seen as strategic, and it has to do with a dominant way of viewing the economic world. Most business people and economists are still disciples (whether they know it or not) of the great post-Enlightenment period of thinking dominated by Newton in the scientific world and Adam Smith in the economic world. To this way of thinking, organizations are—like Newton's universe itself—"well-oiled machines," and the job of business executives is to ensure that a company runs at optimal efficiency. Employees are cogs in the machine and, though some cogs are more important than others, all are replaceable. Although physicists themselves no longer subscribe to Newton's view of the cosmos, business has been slow to follow, and "efficiency" and "productivity" are still the dominant measurements within the human capital paradigm for most organizations. One only has to recall the popularity of business process "reengineering" to realize that is so.

Attitudes toward workforce performance and learning are, therefore, rather entrenched positions at most corporations today, but it was these attitudes that Vanthournout and his team had to confront if they were to be successful driving their vision toward reality. To help change the perception of the value of learning at Accenture, Vanthournout turned to Tad Waddington.

Not your typical Accenture approach

Waddington is, as he himself would be quick to admit, "not your typical Accenture employee." A University of Chicago-trained scholar, Waddington holds a Ph.D. in measurement, evaluation and statistical analysis, and was formerly a research director for the Gallup Organization. Waddington is someone who can drop references to Kant, Plato and Sir Francis Bacon into everyday conversation, along with insights into the measurement of business performance requiring mathematical techniques that most others either do not understand or would prefer to forget. If necessary, he can also do it all in Chinese, in which he is fluent.

The task presented to Waddington was a tall order: give the executives at Accenture a reason to care about learning investments—a reason that goes beyond cost savings and efficiency. Prove to them that the investments they make in learning and human performance translate—in a way no one can question—into improved business performance. And, perhaps just as important, light a fire under them by showing them the potential *negative* impact on the business if they do not make these learning investments.

It was a "not-typical Accenture approach" for this not-typical Accenture employee, but Waddington had, for the past couple of years, been working on a method that showed promise in developing a beyond-reproach return-on-investment model for training. To start, Waddington knew that much of the measurement and ROI language that floats around the business world today cannot withstand much scrutiny. As he bluntly puts it, "Much of the work done in calculating the return on training investments is guilty of misrepresentation. I recall one published report that appeared to prove that a certain course was delivering a 2,000 percent return. The research was done with reasonable rigor, but they had focused on the one course that was of high quality, and not the other 99 percent of the courses. If all courses had an ROI of over 2,000 percent, then we should all just conduct training and retire as millionaires."

Another, more specific issue with regard to creating a believable ROI methodology for training is the overreliance on "soft" data. "At the heart of most training ROI studies is survey data," says Waddington. "'Did you enjoy this course? Would you recommend this course? Did you learn anything?' Consider an analogy: if you're going to assess the performance of a medical staff at a hospital, you'd want to know more than whether a patient was 'satisfied' with the hospital stay. More important questions would be, 'Did the patient survive? Did the problem recur?' A satisfaction score is soft data; what you really want is hard data."

Similarly, says Waddington, "To create a sound ROI model for training, one needs to look beyond operational statistics like numbers of courses, completion rates, total number of students and course satisfaction scores. People sometimes think that if they get a good response to the question, 'Did this experience make you more likely to stay with the company?' that they're getting somewhere. But the hard truth is that you really need to look over time at whether the person did, in fact, stay with the company."

To assess business impact, one also needs to look beyond survey questions such as, "Did this class have an impact on your performance?" "You want to ask the question, to be sure," says Waddington, "but you also need to follow it up with an analysis of the facts. A serious problem in survey research is what is called 'acquiescence bias.' Most people want to be nice and so will answer questions with a 'Yes': 'Yes, this training helped me perform better at my job.'"

However, hard financial data can overcome the bias of soft numbers. A figure like "per-person margin" at Accenture isn't disputable. Says Waddington, "You take a person's billing rate and multiply that by the number of hours the person billed a client. Subtract from that what you pay that person—their cost rate times the number of hours they worked—and you get the hard number of what the person contributed to Accenture's bottom line. Now: can you demonstrate that the financial value the person contributed improved based on the training he or she received? If you can't demonstrate that, you really can't tell anyone you're measuring the business impact of training."

Is there an ROI for learning and training?

The best answers start with the best questions. For the Accenture team, answering the question about the ROI in training had to start by asking if this was even a valid question. Is there a reason to think there is an ROI in this case? "The first law of statistics is that, if something exists, it can be measured," says Waddington. "So our first question was: Does it exist?" According to Waddington, "The integrity of a measurement process really depends on starting from zero. My approach was to begin with the presumption that there is no value to learning. I would not allow us to move in the direction of saying that training has value unless I could defend every step in that direction."

Waddington and a team of researchers began by conducting a comprehensive review of the research literature, examining the relationship between training and business impact. One study conducted by the American Society for Training and Development (ASTD) examined 575 publicly traded companies and made the correlation that every $680 increase in per-employee expenditures in learning opportunities translated into a six-percent improvement in shareholder return for the following year. This study supported a positive answer to the first question: there is reason to believe that training can have an effect on a company's business performance.

Determining ROI for knowledge-intensive companies

This led to the next question: does training have an effect on the business performance of companies that perform knowledge work, and not just manual labor? Most thinking on manufacturing productivity owes a debt to the work of Frederick Taylor, whose classic 1911 book, *The Principles of Scientific Management,* often is given partial credit for the victory by the United States and its allies in World War II. Taylor's principles allowed the allies to simultaneously increase productivity and field more troops. (This also perpetuated the emphasis on "efficiency" mentioned earlier.) Taylor's principles laid the foundation for the modern assembly line, which led to a 50-fold increase in manufacturing productivity in the twentieth century. But Taylor's original study was conducted on a factory floor and involved workers hauling scrap iron. What about workers who haul information and knowledge instead?

Vanthournout, Waddington and team took the step of commissioning an analyst study of Accenture and its competitors to examine the link between learning and business performance.

Although the study was reassuring to the team—it showed that, compared to industry benchmarks, Accenture was providing the most learning opportunities at the lowest cost per hour—the effect of the study went beyond bolstering self-confidence. The research provided further specificity to the ROI agenda for Vanthournout's team, beyond the ASTD study cited previously. This research showed that one must look at more than the *amount* of training spending; this is not the number that drives revenue growth. What matters instead is *the hours of training employees receive*. Think of it as another example like the "satisfaction with hospital stay vs. whether the patient survived" analogy. There is the "medicine" on the one hand and the "result" on the other. "For us," says Waddington, "the medicine isn't the training budget but the hours of training you get for your spending, and the impact of those hours of training on the business. That is, it's not how much you pay for the medicine that matters; it's how much medicine you get and how healthy you are as a result." The result of this study was a positive answer to the second question: in knowledge-intensive companies there is reason to believe that training can have a positive business impact.

Building the ROI model

Now came a third set of questions: in what ways can training have a positive business impact? Through what pathways might training improve a business? To answer these questions, Waddington and team went back to the literature. They learned that there are many ways that training can improve business performance. The literature clearly indicated that one should expect to see beneficial effects in knowledge sharing, increased employee morale, employee networking, recruiting, retention and employee performance.

The challenge, however, was to quantify those business results. There, the team ran into serious difficulties. From course evaluations, classroom observations and interviews with students and their managers, it was clear that one of the biggest effects of training at Accenture was on knowledge sharing. During and after training, people got together and shared what they knew. For months the team worked on ways to quantify the effects of training on knowledge sharing, but came up short. This experience helped the team realize that, while training may lead to a large number of business results, only a subset of those results will be quantifiable. The result of this experience was the creation of a diagram that Waddington calls, "The Egg" (see Figure 1):

Some business measurement studies take what might be called a barrage or "shotgun" approach to what they seek to prove. Pack enough buckshot into a shell and maybe one of the pellets will hit its target. If you can throw enough possible benefits of training and learning out there—on morale, retention, productivity, and on and on—maybe no one will notice that the data to support any particular benefit is shaky. By contrast, Waddington wanted to build a robust ROI model founded only on those elements for which he could find good data. "While the research may indicate that training has broad business impacts," Waddington says, "we were only able to quantify a portion of these. Although this was disappointing, it did mean that our results would be conservative, and, therefore, more believable."

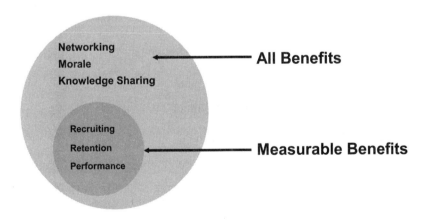

Figure 1. Some benefits of learning can be measured and others cannot

Tying it all together

This last bit of work led to the fourth set of questions: how do all of the pieces fit together? If everything the Accenture team had said was correct, what is the quantifiable model for how training creates business results? Such a model would need to bring everything together without violating what the team had learned in the literature review. "Essentially," said Waddington, "this involved unplugging the phone, drinking a pot of coffee and thinking for a long time." The result was the model shown in Figure 2.

The Y-axis of the model is "contribution," tied to whatever activity is most meaningful to a company and a particular workforce. Sales professionals, for example, can be measured on sales generated; call center professionals can be measured on number of calls handled, inquiries settled or average handling time per call. For Accenture, given the nature of its business and the workforces whose performance were being measured, the research team defined contribution as "per-person margin": bill rate times number of hours billed minus the employee cost over that same time. The X-axis in the diagram represents employees' time with the company. A safe presumption, Waddington believed, is that the longer employees are with the company, the more they contribute. If this were not true, they wouldn't be with

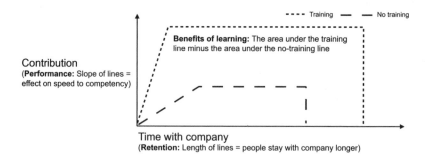

Figure 2. The Accenture Learning ROI Model

the company—particularly in a meritocracy like Accenture, where people in the Consulting workforce are expected either to be able to advance regularly to the next level of responsibility or else leave the organization.

So, imagine two companies, one that provides training and one that does not. The first is represented by the dotted line in the figure; the second, by the dashed line. The ROI literature suggests that training should produce business effects in three ways:

- **It should allow the company with training to hire better employees.** That is, the level of contribution of its employees should be higher than that of a company that does not provide training. Why? Because the company will be more appealing to better people. On the graph, the line representing the company with training is higher than that of the company without training, because of training's positive effect on recruiting.
- **Employees at the company that provides better training opportunities will stay with the company longer than those at the company that does not provide training.** On the graph, the line for the company with training extends further to the right than does that of the company without training, because of training's effects on retention.
- **Employees at the company that provides better training opportunities will achieve competent levels of performance faster than those at the company that does not provide training.** On the graph, the slope of the line for the company that has training is steeper than that of the company that does not, demonstrating the effect of training on performance.

The overall effect of training on the business should be the area under the line for the company that trains minus the area of that for the company that doesn't provide training. "Of course," says Waddington, "this is a simplified conceptual model. The slopes would be different for each individual, as would the overall level of contribution. Also, the lengths of the lines would vary as well. In fact, the lines would be S-curves, and there are other complications, but it serves to guide our thinking. More important, it yields testable predictions."

Testing the model

The model led to a fifth set of questions: how could one know the model was right? How could the Accenture team members be sure they weren't fooling themselves? To answer these questions, the team tested each of the three assumptions of the model.

The effect on recruiting

The team took note of several baseline studies about the effect of learning and training on recruiting. For example, a study of almost 1,000 graduating students and alumni—conducted by the National Association of Colleges and Employers—found that training is among the top three factors (along with benefits packages and the opportunity for advancement) in deciding where one wants to work. More to the point, a survey of more than 2,300 recently hired Accenture employees showed that the opportunity for training and learning was the number-one reason why they had joined Accenture over a competing company. (Recall that this finding also had created a degree of urgency at Accenture for the entire learning reinvention project: if Accenture could not follow through on its promise to recruits to provide effective learning opportunities, it would be perceived as breaching faith with employees.)

So the team had information about the recruits who had accepted an employment offer from Accenture. They also had some data on those who had applied but had not been offered jobs. What they lacked was information about people who might be right for Accenture but who did not apply for employment or had not yet applied. So Waddington and team commissioned a study by a well-known external research organization that surveyed 525 potential recruits at a number of leading American universities. Respondents were not told that Accenture had commissioned the study.

The study asked a series of questions about potential salaries, matched against the three items noted above as the most important factors in deciding to take a job: benefits, advancement and opportunities for learning and training. Suppose, asked the survey, you were offered a job for $45,000 with one company that offered good advancement potential versus another that offered better learning opportunities. Which would you accept? Most respondents chose the company with better learning opportunities. Might they even be willing to take less money now for a job, knowing that the learning programs would offer them better growth potential in the future? Maybe so. Subsequent questions looked for the break point at which they would no longer accept a lower salary: $1,000, $5,000, $10,000.

As it turns out, survey respondents were willing to accept, on average, a salary 13 percent lower than that offered by a competing company, simply on the basis of the perceived excellence of the learning opportunities.

Waddington's conclusions were threefold:

1. People apply to jobs based on advancement opportunities and benefits packages, but if these are roughly equal, they choose among employers based on learning opportunities. Learning programs are the marginal distinction that makes a big difference.

2. Because Accenture, in fact, is comparable with competitors in the salaries offered, it's reasonable to conclude that the company gets better employees for the same cost because of its learning programs. (That is—turning the percentage impact around—one can reasonably say that the people who accepted $45,000 in fact felt they were worth 13 percent more than that.)

3. It is reasonable to hold that a correlation exists between learning and recruiting, a key business driver in the consulting and outsourcing industries.

The effect on retention

The team then turned to the approximately 32,000 responses from Accenture's annual "Employee Satisfaction Survey." One of the questions on this survey asks, "Do you have access at Accenture to the learning opportunities you need to be successful?" Waddington found that employees who did feel they had access to essential learning opportunities were 2.2 times more likely to expect to be with the company in two years, and 6.7 times more likely to think Accenture was "a great place to work." These employees also were more likely to think they were being compensated fairly.

Additional external research also helped make the case for the effect of learning on retention. For example, a reinvigoration of the training programs at the corporate university of a major U.S. airline helped the company to reduce its employee attrition from 18.3 percent to 8.5 percent, producing cost savings of $1.5 million.

These studies suggested that the retention aspect of the model made sense—that there is a relationship between training and business outcomes due to an effect on retention.

The effect on performance

The next step showed why adequate ROI models are so rare: because they require painstaking and arduous attention to detail. Waddington's team combed through course evaluations—evaluations that had been developed over years of research. Waddington's team had met with course sponsors, line partners, course developers, students—anybody interested in the outcome of training—to find out what they wanted to know about courses. Then the team developed end-of-course tests, evaluation items, six-month follow-up surveys with students and their supervisors, and other measures of course success, such as the degree to which course content aligned with business objectives. Every step of the way, the team ran sophisticated psychometric tests to guarantee the statistical quality of the data. At the end of the research, they were able to come up with half a dozen end-of-course survey questions that correlated with stakeholders' interests. As Waddington says, "These are one-size-fits-all questions; none are great, but they do cover what needs covering." In other words, with fairly simple questions, the team could get a rough measure of course quality—a measure that predicted the business performance of the person taking the course.

Waddington's team built these questions into Accenture's new global learning management system (called, "myLearning"—see Chapter 7) so that the team could measure every course Accenture offers. The result? Accenture now has more than 1 million end-of-course evaluations for more than 2,500 courses. Waddington and team found that 85 percent of those who completed the surveys agreed that the training had led to at least a moderate increase in knowledge or skills as a result of taking the course, and 77 percent agreed that the training was applicable to their work. Fifty-three percent held that they had enjoyed a significant increase in productivity due to the training course. Waddington took this result as evidence that the "performance" parameter of the model was sound.

By Waddington's reckoning, however, as important as these numbers were, they were still soft data—merely suggesting relationships between training and business results. The time had come to put the research to the test.

Hard data, hard analyses

The test came with a sixth set of questions: if the ROI model is correct, how does it hold up against rigorous testing? In other words, up to this point the analysis has relied on soft data; but what is the "hard-numbers" answer to the question of the relationship between training and business results?

To assign financial data to this model—making it, then, a statistical model and not just a conceptual one—the team examined the records of more than 261,000 employees containing such data as learning courses completed, cost rates, bill rates, total time with the company and promotions. This data enabled the team to determine per-person margin—defined, again, as the billing rate to clients, multiplied by the number of hours billed minus the cost rate times the hours paid. To ensure that this analysis was as accurate as possible, and to isolate solely the effect of training on performance, Waddington applied regression analysis to factor out other influences such as employee level, months of experience, inflation, the per-hour cost of training and, to some degree, the effects of variable business cycles on Accenture's overall performance.

Was the methodology sound? To cross-check his thinking and the ROI model, Waddington returned to the University of Chicago and to his former professors. They put the model and the results to date to the test. "Are you," one professor asked, "just measuring the intelligence of employees?" In other words, maybe smart people seek out training and do better on the job. "We checked this factor out," recalls Waddington, "using standardized test scores like SATs and grades as proxies. Controlling for these variables, the effect of training on margin was still very clear."

What if, another professor asked, it's the good employees who get to go to training more than their less successful peers? Actually, at Accenture, the situation would be the reverse, if anything. Productive employees from client-facing workforces are those whom senior leadership are often more reluctant to release from their current client work. They perform at higher levels and Accenture's clients tend to want them on site as much as possible.

Finally, Waddington was asked, "How do you know for sure that training is *causing* the business effect?" Waddington said, "We had to be careful with our answer here. Of course we didn't know for certain. We did know that, controlling for all kinds of potential confounds, there is a robust relationship between the amount of training people take and their contribution to the company. We have good reason, based on our theory, to think the relationship is causal, but many very smart people have been unable to prove causality beyond a shadow of a doubt."

"Good enough," the professors finally said. In fact, they concluded that they could see no flaws in the research, the methodology or the conclusions.

And, the results

"Conducting statistical analysis," Waddington says, "ended up being quite simple, because no matter what we did, we kept getting the same answer. It was very robust." The team used the total hours of training employees had received as an independent variable. They controlled for factors that might confound the relationship, such as experience, inflation and business cycle. And they used "employee contribution" as the outcome or dependent variable. This allowed them to calculate the effect of training on contribution while controlling for factors that might cloud the picture.

The result was that the annual net benefit of learning was $25,324 per Accenture employee. Multiplying that figure by the number of Accenture consulting employees at the time of the analysis (about 50,000) yielded a companywide net benefit from training of $1.27 billion, or about 11 percent of Accenture revenues at that time.

With this big-picture understanding of the data, the team could then calculate the effects of training on different aspects of the business. The team found that employees in the top fiftieth percentile of training—that is, employees who take more learning offerings have the following characteristics:

- They are 17 percent more "chargeable" to Accenture's clients. This translates into an additional value to Accenture of $8,400 per person.
- They have 20 percent higher billing rates to clients. This was worth about $9,900 per person to Accenture. In the long run, this effect is due to the fact that these employees are promoted. (Interestingly, on average, highly trained employees reach the next level of promotion 28 days *later* than less highly trained employees, but reach higher levels in the long run.)

- They stay with the company 14 percent longer. That longevity translates into about $7,000 of additional value per person annually to Accenture.

The overall formula guiding Waddington and the team for coming up with a final return on learning number was:

- ROI = Net Benefit/Cost

With the help of Accenture's finance team, Waddington calculated that the non-payroll costs that roll up into training expenses totaled $358 million. The net benefit of training was, therefore, $1.27 billion. To calculate final ROI, they simply divided the net benefit of $1,266,215,414 by $358,366,376.

The answer: 353 percent.

This was a number that Vanthournout and Waddington could take to their steering committee, to the CEO and board of directors, and to the outside world of investors—a number that would speak loudly and clearly. Take a dollar; invest it in learning programs for the company; you'll get back $4.53 (that is, your original dollar plus an additional $3.53).

This was a critical moment in the reinvention of training and learning at Accenture—critical to achieving that stated goal of making learning "one of the top three initiatives for the company." The ROI number said, "This stuff is important. Learning investments are not just the 'right thing to do' for our people. They make strong financial sense."

Going beyond: the total impact of learning

Accenture's model of learning ROI was not only academically verified; it also won a number of subsequent awards, including a Corporate University Xchange Excellence for Measurement award, a Gold Excellence in E-Learning Measurement award from Brandon Hall, and two awards from the American Society for Training and Development.

Versions of Accenture's ROI model also were subsequently applied successfully at a number of other companies, including a major telecommunications company. There, training and knowledge management programs led to a doubling of sales conversion rates for call center agents, a 16 percent increase in customer satisfaction and a 50 percent reduction in overall training costs.

Yet the Accenture team also knew that the learning ROI work now needed to be applied to current work and future planning, to ensure that learning programs continually evolved to meet the company's changing business needs. By combining what they learned from the ROI study and the end-of-course evaluation data, for example, the team can now estimate the ROI of every course they offer. But the ROI work also has helped them understand the more holistic effects of learning on Accenture's culture and its business performance.

"One of our key insights from this ROI work," says Vanthournout, "was that the effects of learning on business performance are cumulative over time. Any single course by itself is unlikely to have much of a discernible effect. But when you look at several courses in conjunction with each other, you begin to see measurable impacts." Waddington elaborates, "People who have tried to measure the business impact of learning have sought to measure ROI by looking at how a specific course taught specific skills to specific individuals. Doing it that way, it is almost statistically impossible to measure how an individual course has a business impact. You have to look at the big picture of training—how all of the courses work in concert with each other."

In presentations he delivers about Accenture's "return on learning" research, Waddington likes to illustrate the role of learning in organizational success by showing his audience what is called a "photo mosaic." These are pictures that appear at first to be of a single subject: a human face, perhaps, or a landscape. On close inspection, however, the photos actually are mosaics of hundreds of smaller photos, digitally analyzed for their color content and placed appropriately on a larger canvas to create the bigger picture. The lesson: the value of learning goes far beyond the simpler cause and effect of a person or group taking a single course.

"The effects of learning on organizational value," says Waddington, "are cumulative. Any single learning or training event is unlikely to have a dramatic effect on the organization. But the effects of many people and many events interacting with each other and the knowledge of the entire company begins to add up to create the bigger picture."

So decision makers who focus on the value of individual courses and ignore how various learning experiences interact with each other risk underestimating the true value of learning, in the same way that looking just at the book value of an asset can lead one to underestimate market capitalization. "Learning has pervasive effects," Waddington concludes. "Its value is greater than the sum of the parts."

- Obtaining effective executive buy-in and sponsorship for learning programs depends on giving executives convincing proof of the business benefits.
- Learning professionals and other workforce performance experts cannot presume that executive leadership understands or truly believes that the workforce is a distinctive contributor to business excellence. They may need to be convinced.
- Through metrics and ROI analysis, learning investments can be linked to business performance outcomes.
- In conducting an ROI analysis, organizations should focus less on soft data such as course evaluations and more on how learning improved a person's performance on the job.
- To measure the value of learning, organizations should seek to measure all of the programs, not just a course here and there. This also prevents the mistake of getting false results by focusing only on the best (or worst) courses.
- It's not how much organizations spend on learning programs that matters; it's how much benefit they get out of those expenditures.

Four

The Leadership to Succeed

One of the paradoxes of corporate learning—and, indeed, of any initiative focused on transforming and renewing an organization's workforce—is that learning is both extremely important and also easy to overlook or take for granted. Information technology professionals often gripe that no one notices anything they do until a server goes down, and human resources and learning professionals face much the same situation. Sure, learning programs can be a lure for a company like Accenture to attract the best recruits, but after the first couple of years, additional learning opportunities become part of the general background of the company—maybe even a distraction from the important business of making profits and moving up the corporate ladder.

Thus, the distinctive value of learning is something that must be constantly articulated and justified within an organization. The business case for learning must be updated regularly. And senior leadership must be continually reminded that the company is in the knowledge business. When a company's competitive advantage resides primarily in the individual and collective brains of its employees, it's the learning programs that determine whether the "product" is going to have ongoing value in the marketplace.

Sustained executive interest is what matters most when it comes to investments in learning. As seen in the previous chapter, the Accenture team had taken one crucial step toward winning sustained executive interest in the reinvention of learning for business impact at Accenture: they had shown that training was not just a cost center or a budgetary drain. They had the statistics to show both the threats and the opportunities. They had shown what had happened to Accenture when executive leadership had failed to sustain its learning investments and broken its "learning deal" with employees; but they also had produced a rigorous study showing the business upside of learning investments—a 353 percent return on learning.

Perhaps most important, they had taken the time to validate their findings externally. It's possible to ignore or overlook some internal Ph.D.-type who claims to have important research findings; it's harder to overlook an internationally renowned thought leader who's talking about the research, or editors from major business magazines who come calling to discuss the metrics program, or a major industry award affirming the value of the work. At the very least, Accenture leadership was saying to Vanthournout and his team, "OK. You have our attention."

A model for effective journey management

Beginning in the early 1990s, Accenture had begun to develop and perfect a rich set of methodologies and processes for helping its clients manage over time the complicated organizational effects of large, complex technology and process reengineering projects. Clients were looking to Accenture for help in delivering projects on time and on budget, and in reaping the full long-term value of their investments. This was a period marked in particular by the recognition that swift marketplace change and intense competition were requiring new ways to move an entire organization through major change. Executives in both the private and public sector had grown increasingly frustrated with failed strategic initiatives—failures that resulted in large part because corporate cultures could not or would not embrace the change.

Many corporate education departments began to retool or augment their learning offerings with what was often called "technology assimilation" training. Technology was driving new ways of working. People needed help assimilating new technology and learning to work with it, and the technology systems themselves had to be designed with usability in mind. Corporate education departments became concerned with more than just training for new hires or about new products, or creating courses related to basic functions like selling and customer service. Companies were starting to realize that their multimillion-dollar information systems were not going to return much on their investment unless greater focus was placed on the people who actually used those systems.

But such an approach could only go so far. In the end, it simply forced change on people, and did little to create a desire for change within the corporate culture. To create an environment in which change would face less resistance from an organization's people, both academics and practitioners of "change management" began to develop more sophisticated methods and tools. Executives started becoming more comfortable with different ways of thinking about business problems and opportunities: not organizations as machines, but as complex ecosystems; not people as only resources to be mined, but as potential value creators for the entire organization.

Organizations also began to use the metaphor of a journey for their major change programs. A simple "A to B" straight line, based on simplistic cause-and-effect relationships, could not adequately capture the challenges of organizational change. (See accompanying box on understanding and managing the journey of transformation change.) It was this awareness of the overall transformational nature of Accenture's reinvention of learning that led to a sophisticated and innovative structure to help achieve leadership and sponsorship of change. This framework helped the training organization itself accomplish ownership of the change, and helped put in place a governance structure that could smooth the journey ahead.

Behind the leadership and governance program was the strong desire to do more than win in the short term—to do more than just arrive at a destination and celebrate. The team was after greater sustained leadership and cultural change at Accenture. Notes Vanthournout, "We had a shared vision with our leadership team from day one, and we used that vision to keep everyone together on the journey. We didn't let them off the hook once we had a strategy. We said, 'No: you helped us develop the strategy, but now we're walking along this path together. You can't leave now.'"

Even a successful organizational change journey has its risks: in particular, the risk that the change will not be sustained because leadership attention will have moved on to the "next big thing." Says Vanthournout, "It's one thing to get management's attention when you have a major problem to solve. It's another to sustain that attention so that an organization doesn't backslide. Companies that have successfully managed a change journey sometimes forget to focus on how to keep management from simply moving on to the next set of really big problems. In effect, the journey to transform your culture and your human capital is never over. Everyone needs to say, 'Yes, we've accomplished some great things, but the journey isn't over.'"

A framework for understanding and managing transformational change

Many models, tools and techniques have arisen in recent years to help organize and manage the different components of major organizational change. The Accenture Journey Framework provides a simple yet powerful way to communicate to company executives the most important categories of work that must be done to ensure that a workforce both can and will perform over the course of a major program of organizational change: in other words, accomplish a program that is transformational and not just tactical. The journey framework divides organizational change issues and challenges into four categories, along two important axes. The first axis is supply versus demand. That is, organizations must attend not only to programs that "push" the change initiatives, but also to programs that create a "pull" for the change from within the workforce itself. The second axis is macro versus micro. That is, major change requires both high-level programs that affect the entire organization and programs that touch individuals.

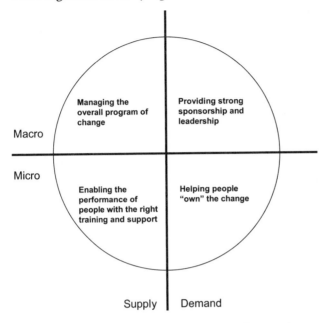

Macro

Micro

Managing the overall program of change	Providing strong sponsorship and leadership
Enabling the performance of people with the right training and support	Helping people "own" the change

Supply | Demand

Managing a journey of change: The Accenture Journey Framework

The two axes result in four major types of initiatives that can increase the chances of success on the change journey:

- **Leadership.** Activities that develop and nurture executives who will support and sponsor the change initiative.
- **Ownership.** Actions designed to ensure that the entire corporate culture accepts the changes and will continue to be motivated to high levels of performance during the change.
- **Enablement.** Training, education, knowledge management and other related activities that provide the workforce with the capability to perform at high levels.
- **Navigation.** Management activities dedicated to overseeing the many different strands of a change program.

Governance, leadership and sponsorship at two levels

An innovative approach taken by the Accenture team was to ensure that governance structures and sponsorship initiatives for the change program were instituted at two levels. Kurt Olson, who led the detailed development of the new learning curricula as part of the reinvention program, recalls, "Early on, we took note that our success was going to be based on the ongoing commitment and involvement both of the executives who controlled budgets and business priorities, and of the executives with vested interests in making sure their parts of the organization, and their services and offerings, were represented in the learning content."

No learning program will ever be able to accomplish everything, meet everyone's expectations and serve everyone's needs. Effective governance of a learning transformation program must win the hearts and minds of those leading the organization at the highest level, as well as those more directly involved in detailed business strategies and the training necessary to make those strategies successful. "Most of the time," says Olson, "organizations will have a five-pound bag of training available, but ten pounds of content for the bag. So they need to have in place the process to manage that content down to get the right five pounds into the bag. Governance is needed from a broad and high perspective, but it is also needed from a content and course perspective."

However, the decision on content and courses did not occur in a vacuum at Accenture. John Ceisel—Kurt Olson's lead for the team that defined core skills for Accenture's Consulting workforce, corporate compliance and sales courses—highlights the business rigor in the decisions presented to the steering committee. "The number of hours and non-payroll expenses were financially modeled to ensure that the costs were viable within Accenture's cost and profitability models. This business rigor, says Ceisel, "was key to addressing stakeholder concerns about affordability."

The executive steering committee

The steering committee put in place to lead and sponsor a major change program must reflect the organization's unique reporting and go-to-market structures. In the case of Accenture, Smart and Vanthournout made plans for a steering committee that would include all major stakeholders within the company—the chief executives of all the major functional and business groups within the company.

Accenture goes to market primarily through what it calls "operating groups." These are groups with deep specialty skills and experience in particular industries and subindustries, organized at the highest level into five areas: Communications and High Tech, Financial Services, Resources, Products and Government. In addition, however, each employee specializes in a particular capability, and so the organization also organizes its people and work according to those capabilities: technology, strategy, financial management, human performance, customer relationship management and so forth. Thus, any particular employee in the Consulting workforce is a member of an operating group (reflecting deep knowledge of an industry) and simultaneously a member of a capability group (reflecting deep knowledge of a specialized domain).

The chief executives for each of the five operating groups, as well as the leads for the capability groups, were appointed to the steering committee for the learning transformation program, as was the company's chief leadership officer. With Jill Smart present as the senior managing director of human resources, and Don Vanthournout as the head of learning, the steering committee was complete.

The kinds of meetings a steering committee like this has will change as a transformation program proceeds. At the beginning of the Accenture program, meetings were often held in person as the team "hammered out the strategy," as Vanthournout puts it. "At the start," he notes, "personal interaction is absolutely critical to the successful governance of a program. You need to do more than discuss the kinds of 'official' strategy documents that the top executives sanction. You need to hear those strategies come to life in the actual words of your company's top stakeholders. In our case we needed to hear not only the official statements, but also what was on their minds—how they were interpreting the strategy and how they were going to bring it alive to our customers and our employees, and where they intended to take the company in the long run."

Smart echoes the importance of the steering committee to the learning transformation program. "The sponsorship of our executive steering committee was so important that 'sponsorship' itself really isn't a strong enough word. What an organization needs at a time like this is a form of activity from leadership that goes beyond support or cheerleading and becomes active participation. That made the difference. And it especially made a difference when the economy continued to spiral downward. There were some who wanted to cut back on our learning services yet again, but the group chief executives—who were by then sponsors of the core schools—said, 'No. If we're going to serve our clients well, if we're going to be innovative and conduct high-quality work, our people have to be at the leading edge of their fields.'"

An effective steering committee is also one that sticks to its plans and promises and uses its clout wisely, when needed, to push past resistance. The decisions made by such a group at a company like Accenture generally have hefty price tags attached to them. Here is one example. As discussed in Chapter 2, Accenture leadership had affirmed from the start the desire to gradually return Accenture's learning programs back to a modified version of the "core" training that had, at one point, characterized the distinctive Accenture approach to enterprise learning. As a first step, the team made sure that new hires (called "analysts") went to their first core school within six to 12 months after joining the company. Eventually, however, based on the evolution of the company's business strategy, the decision-makers felt it was appropriate to move that back to when employees start their jobs, just as it had once been for the company.

Vanthournout recalls, "Even though we were unanimous on the steering committee that this was the right decision, I had to go to them and let them know that it was a $20 million decision. We had more than 3,600 analysts that we were going to have to catch up to get them in synch with the shift in timing of this course, and that was going to be the price tag. It was up to the steering committee to authorize the means to pay for it."

And then, of course, that budget decision rippled through and temporarily disappointed some other people in the organization, because their learning programs or specialty areas would lose funding for a time until the analysts caught up with the timing of the core school. "But having a strong steering committee made it easier for everyone—and certainly for us in the internal training and HR organization," says Vanthournout. "I didn't need to convince hundreds of people myself that it was the right thing to do. I could just say, 'Hey, I talked to your group chief executive and this is what he or she wants to do.' It doesn't mean contrary opinions don't exist or aren't welcome. It just means that, when hard decisions have to be made, the executives are prepared to be accountable for their decisions and to stick with them."

Building effective sponsorship of change

Multilevel executive sponsorship is an important element of all change programs. Strong sponsorship starts at the top. To execute a transformational change program, companies must identify leaders who are well-respected, who support and communicate the vision of the transformation, who provide the resources necessary to make the program successful and who help institutionalize the change throughout the organization.

Sponsorship is not the responsibility of one person, but of representatives of the entire organization—something that can be called a "sponsor network."

Based on Accenture's experiences in supporting major change

programs for clients, the following are key steps to bear in mind when creating and managing an effective sponsorship program.

- **Develop the sponsorship plan.** The sponsorship plan describes the required levels of sponsorship, the roles and responsibilities of the sponsors, and an approach for implementing and sustaining the sponsor network. When designing the sponsorship plan, the overall program management team for the change program must consider the variety of operating units, locations, countries and functions involved in the program. The plan must define the best way to engage sponsors, taking into account their job level, location and schedules. Engagement options include one-on-one meetings, group meetings and conference calls or written communications.

- **Define the nature of sponsor commitment.** While the sponsor network must include members from all levels across the organization, the sponsors will not have unlimited time to help advance the change agenda. The best sponsorship approach will provide sponsors with a clear understanding of their roles and levels of commitment so that they can manage their time accordingly.

- **Define the sponsorship-tracking approach.** Effective sponsorship of change is not a "soft" activity. Sponsorship activities must be formally planned and managed. Successful sponsorship efforts use a formal tracking tool to help manage the status of the activities and interactions.

- **Identify and recruit sponsors.** Once the sponsorship plan is approved, the program management team must identify and recruit sponsors. The requestors must clearly communicate the importance and far-reaching implementation challenges of the transformation and position the role of a sponsor appropriately.

- **Launch sponsorship activity.** The program will be launched by formally engaging the targeted sponsors to begin building awareness.

- **Manage sponsor network.** When the sponsorship activity has been launched, the sponsorship plan must be implemented, engaging individual sponsors or groups of sponsors as defined. Sponsorship management is critical at each phase of a transformation program.

Keys to success

- Select sponsors who have a track record for driving change, providing access to the required resources and garnering organizational respect.
- Select a range of sponsors that provide an adequate level of coverage across operating units, countries, functions and so forth.
- "Cascade" sponsorship to ensure all levels of the organization are kept informed of developments.
- Estimate the time that sponsors must commit to the project. Most candidates for a sponsor role have many responsibilities within an organization; ensure that anyone chosen for this role can commit the time needed to provide the required level of support.
- During the course of the project, a sponsor may not have the required impact, or may take on a different role within the organization. There should be a process in place for identifying and selecting new sponsors, and bringing them up to speed quickly.

Aligning training content with business need

As noted, another key to the success of the learning transformation program at Accenture was the second level of governance put in place to drive the creation of learning content tied closely to the most current business objectives of the company. This second level was achieved by designating executive sponsors for each course in the evolving curriculum. In most cases these sponsors were selected from members of the steering committee. This approach gave members of the steering committee an additional personal ownership in the quality of the learning experience.

For Vanthournout and team, this level of governance was critical to strengthening the connection between the learning organization and the needs of Accenture's business. In Jill Smart's words, "It's best when the learning organization sees itself as the production line creating the product, but then gives the business owners responsibility for designing what the product should look like. By analogy, it's as if the business owners should be telling us what the car should look like when it comes off the assembly line, but then I and my team will work to produce a great car at the right price."

The business owners have to help define the learning content in order to keep learning services aligned with business need. So a governance structure that involves those business owners is critical to achieving the best return on learning.

Overseeing the development of the learning content itself at Accenture was largely the responsibility of Kurt Olson. As Olson recalls, the process of developing new learning programs could have been so complex as to derail the entire team. But, partly at the urging of Smart, the team began to develop learning content with what came to be called simply "one-pagers." Recalls Olson, "The concept of these one-pagers was deceptively simple, but they were actually crucial to our success. We began with five sheets of paper, one for each of the levels of our employees in the Consulting workforce: analysts, consultants, managers, senior managers and partners. The goal of the executive in charge of each major content area was to summarize on that single page what the performance outcomes needed to be as employees progressed through various career levels. Then we negotiated with the content owners how to organize the content, how to present it according to career development stages, and how to deliver the learning experience most effectively at each stage, whether that experience was in the classroom or on the Web."

This planning process also helped to define what would be

"core" learning and what would be covered by specialty or ad hoc courses. For example, for the Consulting workforce, five areas of content were defined for the core learning programs:

- Leadership and culture
- Business processes, acumen and value creation
- Relationship building, effective communications and selling
- Management disciplines (such as program and project management)
- Solution delivery, technology acumen, quality and methods

This was a crucial phase for the team. It returned Accenture to the days when core training, in pursuit of common excellence and a shared culture, dominated the training curriculum. At the same time, the approach provided focus so that less investment money was wasted sending employees to learning programs for which they had no need. Everyone received common training in core skills; then, only those with a need for specialized industry or capability training attended those courses.

Once there had been socialization of the idea that the core curriculum would be required for all people in a workforce, there were many groups that wanted to ensure that their content was a part of the core courses. To manage the limited space available for content in the core curriculum, it was necessary to develop a broader curriculum framework. This framework enabled Vanthournout's team to have discussions with various content sponsors about the best place for their content. What this meant for the learning transformation program is that the team did not have to say, "No, your content does not get to go in the core curriculum." Instead, they could say, "Your content does not go into the core because there is another place in the overall curriculum that is a better fit for your content, based on the intended audience."

In addition to the core curriculum, several other components of the curriculum framework were defined and sanctioned by the steering committee. These supported the development of deeper industry and specialty skills in the targeted audiences that required these skills. The framework also provided room for "just-in-time" training to prepare employees for specific roles they were about to undertake, and also accommodated community meetings, where employees from a regional area could gather to socialize, hear communications from leadership and learn from each other. All these components came together in the development of a unique curriculum framework for each of the four workforces (the Consulting workforce framework is shown in Figure 1).

"The curriculum frameworks gave us the structure to immediately begin delivering higher-quality training with greater cost efficiency," says Olson. "We could ask, for example, 'OK, for this

Analyst	Consultant	Manager	Senior Manager	Senior Executive
Core Training				
New Joiner Orientation				
Solution Delivery Fundamentals	Core Consultant/ Specialist Milestone	Core Manager/ Level B Milestone	Core Sr. Manager/ Level A Milestone	The Accenture Selling Platform
Core Analyst School	Core Consultant School	Core Manager School	Core Sr. Manager School	
Leadership & Culture				
Business Processes, Acumen & Value Creation				
Relationship Building & Selling				
Management Disciplines				
Solution Delivery, Technology Acumen, Quality & Methodology				
Service Line Training	Consultant Service Line Program	Manager Service Line Program	Sr. Mgr. Service Line Program	Sr. Exec. Service Line Program
		Offerings, Value, Positioning, Integration		
		Domain / Specialty, Offering Specialization		
	Offerings Overview, Fundamentals			
Industry Training			Industry Value Targeting	
		Industry Value Levers, Offerings		
	Industry Overviews / Fundamentals			
Professional and Job Readiness Training				
		Leadership & Personal Development Electives		
	Business Courses & Self Study			
	Program/Project Management Electives			
	Job Readiness Courses			
Community Meetings				
	Value Creator			
	Business Operator			
	People Developer			

Figure 1. The Accenture Curriculum Framework for the Consulting workforce

content and this performance outcome, do you really need to fly people to a central location for classroom training and use up expensive executive time for teaching? Or, could this be done virtually or through an e-learning solution?' With the right governance system in place for content design and delivery, we could effectively give the content decisions to the school sponsors who were closest to the need, while maintaining control over how the content would be delivered to maximize the effectiveness of the experience while also staying within our cost constraints."

"Locking in" learning services and strategy

Keeping learning services aligned with the needs of a business or government agency is on the minds of most senior executives today. What organizations need is a way to ensure close collaboration between those responsible for the development and delivery of learning content and those senior managers responsible for establishing business goals and objectives. This ongoing alignment is too important to be left to chance or to informally "keeping management informed." Companies need a more formal organizational structure and system of governance to ensure that strategy and workforce enablement are "locked in." Indeed, at Accenture we call this structure "Business Interlock": a business function with services, interactions, metrics and application capabilities that link learning outcomes to business objectives.

The Accenture Business Interlock governance approach operates on a few critical guiding principles:

- Ensure senior executives understand learning and performance needs, issues with learning delivery and how learning can improve the results of the business.
- Facilitate an annual planning process and quarterly demand forecasts around learning demand, capability and affordability.
- Establish a single point of contact for all learning and performance requests from the business.
- Structure more effective communication channels

between the business and the corporate learning organization.

- Ensure participation of the learning organization in the overall governance process.

Business Interlock does not simply add another step in the learning supply chain of content sourcing, cataloging, delivery and administration. It transforms the supply chain in the same way that new processes transformed the manufacturing supply chain to enable just-in-time manufacturing. In fact, that's the ultimate goal of Business Interlock: a just-in-time approach to learning.

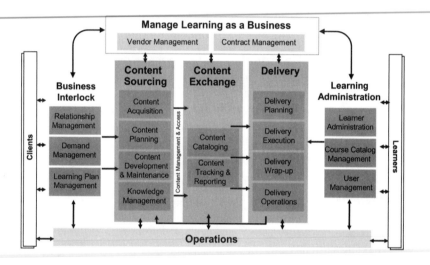

The Accenture Business Interlock governance approach

Three elements form the heart of the Accenture Business Interlock governance approach:

1. Understanding the business.
2. Directing the impact that learning has on business results.
3. Managing relationships with key decision makers and being included in their agendas from a planning and business management perspective.

Understanding the business

You can't steer a ship from the bow; the rudder has to be back at the stern. In the same way, steering the learning organization depends on understanding the business well enough so that learning decision makers can be among those sitting in the pilot's seat—which means earlier in the product development or organizational strategy cycles. For example, consider the benefit of involving learning professionals as part of the development process for new products. Done properly, this means that when the product is ready for market, the training is ready to enable the workforce to sell it. This is "learning plan management," to be sure, but not in the traditional sense. Given the constraints on the learning supply chain flexibility, this approach provides anticipatory management. It runs not just in parallel with business planning, but integrated with it.

Directing the learning results

Business Interlock gives organizations the kind of demand management structures that provide fact-based decision mechanisms. Learning outcomes do not have to be fuzzy, but can result from hard, fact-based questions: what are the budget numbers? What are the results you're looking for from your workforce and therefore from the business? What priorities must be made given the balance of desired results and resource constraints? With Business Interlock, one can avoid the two most common mistakes organizations make with workforce enablement: 1) They underestimate the costs and then have to find ways to skimp; or 2) They cut out the enablement part completely—which means the business fails to realize the practical benefits the project was supposed to provide in the first place. One way that Business Interlock provides better management is by creating good database metrics and planning tools, to provide for easier and more accurate estimating and planning of resource allocation and strategy execution.

Managing relationships

Part of good relationship management is planning and developing communications with the business users or workforce whose performance is critical to the company's strategic mission. The other part, however, is the management of relationships with key decision makers. Again, the learning function has to be among those sitting in the pilot's chair of the ship. And that can't happen by accident, or only through persuasion and cajoling. It needs to be built into the governance structures of the company. Leaders must institutionalize mechanisms that ensure enablement and strategy are developed hand in hand. In the end, structure drives process, not the other way around.

At this point in Accenture's learning transformation journey, Vanthournout and his team had a learning strategy in place, and they had a detailed set of blueprints for the learning programs required to meet the needs of Accenture employees from different workforces at different stages in their careers. Now the task would be to create learning experiences with maximum impact on workforce performance. The team would soon have a name for those kinds of learning experiences: "phenomenal learning."

- Senior leadership must be continually reminded that, if a company is in the knowledge business—if its competitive advantage resides primarily in the individual and collective brains of its employees—it's the learning programs that determine whether the "product" is going to have ongoing value in the marketplace.
- Reinvigorating the enterprise learning capability for any organization is an exercise in journey management.
- Effective governance is not just about reaching the destination—it's also about sustaining the success over time. If management attention wavers, a company can backslide.
- Effective governance of a transformation program must win the hearts and minds of those steering the ship at the highest level, as well as those more directly involved in detailed business strategies and the learning programs necessary to make those strategies successful.
- The steering committee put in place to lead and sponsor a major change program must reflect the unique reporting and go-to-market structures of the organization.
- The types and frequency of steering committee meetings will change over time, as needs dictate and as the nature of the overall transformation journey changes.
- An effective steering committee sticks to its plans and promises, and uses its clout wisely when needed to push past resistance.
- The learning function and business owners must work hand in hand: the business owners make sure the content is in alignment with the business needs, and the learning function makes sure that the learning experiences produced are high-quality and cost effective.

Five

Phenomenal Learning

The Accenture team had a good grasp now of *what* needed to go into its redesigned learning programs—the content to support the business as well as the individual performance needs of people at different stages of their careers. The team also had a plan for *how* those learning programs were to be delivered—the mix of classroom and electronic learning appropriate both to the budget and to the performance need that the learning was to support. Now the team had to deal with a lingering issue that had awaited them from the start. How would they reconcile the economic reality at Accenture with the high expectations for the quality of the courses?

Recall that the walls and offices of Accenture's training organization were filled with awards for innovative training programs, the spoils of an earlier era when the focus had been more on innovative learning design and delivery than on business alignment and operational efficiency. Accenture employees had very high expectations for the quality of Accenture learning experiences. As a leader in delivering advanced learning to clients, Accenture had a reputation to uphold. And Vanthournout's team had its own sense of pride, and a strong desire not to see satisfaction surveys come back that said quality had deteriorated on their watch. Those factors added up to a bar that was raised very high already. The team's response: let's raise it higher.

It was Jill Smart who provided the label for what they wanted to accomplish. During one of their team meetings early in the learning transformation journey, Smart remarked, "Whatever else we do, the learning programs we create have to be *phenomenal*." The word stuck.

The experience of learning

The "phenomenal" label as the summary vision for learning design and delivery at Accenture caught on for more reasons than simply because it was the boss who had come up with it. In addition to being slang for "absolutely off-the-charts great," "phenomenal" also tapped into a major business trend in how to differentiate a company and keep its products from becoming commoditized: the move to a mindset of delivering "experiences" to customers and not just services. For Accenture, the new learning programs were not just about the content—the information to be covered and mastered—but also the "phenomena" surrounding the delivery of a course and the learning experience.

Accenture has conducted research into the kinds of customer contact experiences that are characteristic of high-performance businesses. One of the research findings is that the best companies all focus on delivering a "branded" experience. At every customer touchpoint, high-performance businesses know that their brand is constantly on the line; a customer service representative interacting with a customer does, in fact, represent the entire company. Similarly, an employee taking a learning program—whether in person at the St. Charles campus or online—is experiencing the Accenture brand: the value the company stands for, its image in the marketplace and the type of culture that binds together its people.

What exactly is the value of an "experience"? In their book *The Experience Economy,* authors Joseph Pine and James Gilmore ask that organizations think of experiences as a fourth kind of economic offering, in addition to commodities, goods and services. An experience is more than a service; the associations or "phenomena" that come along with the service are also important. An experience is an immersive, richly textured commercial event.

People who buy a service are actually purchasing a set of intangible experiences carried out on their behalf. But people buying experiences are paying "to spend time enjoying a series of memorable events that a company stages—as in a theatrical play—to engage [people] in a personal way."[1]

Disney—both the man himself and the company that bears his name—is acknowledged by many as the patron saint of the business trend toward delivering experiences to customers and not just services. Visitors to Disney World, Disneyland or Euro Disney are visiting "theme" parks; they are guests, not customers. People who work for the parks are creating experiences for guests, not delivering services; they are "cast members," not employees. Today, many of the most successful company brands are built on the delivery of differentiated customer experiences. From Starbucks (where a relatively small percentage of the cost of a skim latte is related to the price of coffee beans, and the rest is related to the experience of receiving a custom-made cup of coffee) to JetBlue (the low-cost airline where each employee is considered to be a "crewmember," and every customer sits in a leather seat and has access to 24 channels of DIRECTV programming), companies are striving to deliver experiences that one economist has called "festive"[2]—experiences that take customers out of their routine lives and give them a good reason to come back again and again.

The Disney-type experiential model was very much on the minds of the Accenture team. In the movie *Matilda,* the shrewish elementary school principal places signs in every classroom that read, "If you are having fun, you are not learning." But leading practitioners of corporate education know otherwise. They know the importance of *engaging* the adult learner to bring about the true behavior change that is the goal of enterprise learning. Phenomenal or experiential learning, according to the Accenture team, should aim to engage the learner in a way that creates the desired behaviors and also strengthens the bond between the employee and the company.

Reviews of Accenture courses even came to be called "phenomenality reviews." These reviews focused on more than whether people simply learned what they were intended to learn. Recalls Vanthournout, "The reviews gave us the data we needed to become even more aggressive in delivering phenomenal learning. The question became, what else can we do to create a learning experience here that has the potential to change someone's career—even change someone's life? For those employees already satisfied with their work, what can we do to make them feel even better about working for Accenture? And for those whose commitment to the company is wavering, how can we have them go home from a training class in St. Charles saying, 'Why would I ever think about leaving this company?'"

Defining and delivering phenomenal learning

Beyond the slogan, though, what exactly is a "phenomenal" learning experience and what are the more mundane structures and delivery mechanisms necessary to make it happen? The Accenture team came up with a short definition to serve as a beacon during course design and development: phenomenal learning meant "creating a surprising and delighting level of excellence in every aspect of the training experience."

The team quickly found that they could not address the challenge of phenomenal learning without touching on the complex topic of *emotion.* Says Kurt Olson, "We had to work to overcome the somewhat natural aversion business people have to the idea of emotion. Ultimately, we told our curriculum planners and course designers that they had to build some form of emotional experience into a course. We worked to create an emotional connectedness—the kind of fiber that binds people together at work. What we wanted was for a group to walk away from a week of training at St. Charles with a broader network—a couple dozen new colleagues who they know—just *know*—they can always count on and can call if they get in trouble or just need a good word."

So, although the overall direction of where the team wanted to go with phenomenal learning was clear, a question remained: who is actually responsible for creating a phenomenal learning experience? One answer is that it's a combination of designers, developers and sponsors. However, two additional critical roles need to be highlighted. One is the Business Interlock role highlighted in the previous chapter. That role, also referred to within Vanthournout's group as a "solution planner," is essential for curriculum planning. As Olson notes, exceptional solution planners form the linchpin for making phenomenal learning a reality, because they sit at the intersection of content sponsors, curriculum sponsors, instructional designers and the faculty. Solution planners are charged with understanding the business—ensuring that learning achieves the business results, and also managing the multiple decision makers involved in the learning process. Notes Olson, "Ultimately, these are business professionals who happen to be working in the learning space, mixing value creation and business operations in day-to-day decision making. We set the bar very high for the development of phenomenal learning, yet we also were looking to take hundreds of millions of dollars out of the cost equation for learning. Our solution planners were the ones charged with making that happen."

A second critical role, according to Olson, is played by the executives who serve as teaching faculty. Part of delivering phenomenal learning meant increasing the commitment of Accenture's executives to teach in St. Charles again. Jill Smart notes that, "One of the key success factors for our classroom learning is that we minimized our use of outside faculty. Yes, the good thing about trained, experienced faculty is that you increase your chances that every teaching moment will be high-quality and branded. However, having our own executives there as faculty was also necessary to the experience. That executive commitment said something essential about our culture. It said that our leaders care enough about our employees to take time away from their client work to be there up in front of the classroom. When you have your own executives teaching, it means that the learning experiences continue outside the classroom, outside the formal curriculum. When the teacher and students go to lunch or to the social center in the evening, the learning experience goes on."

Defining the entire milieu of learning and the entire scope of its influence was an important part of Accenture's definition of phenomenal learning. Kurt Olson notes that the team's increasing comfort level with the "experience" economy meant that they saw their scope as going far beyond the classroom or online course itself. "The training experience actually starts with the very first contact that an employee has with Accenture; it ends only if a person leaves the company. We now see our domain as touching an employee's entire experience with Accenture—the learning experience and the Accenture enculturation experience, as well as what Disney would call the 'guest' experience. The 'excellence' we refer to in our definition of phenomenal learning has to do with the brand associations of professionalism, care, consideration and quality that come to mind based on the entire experience." This doesn't mean, Olson says, that the course development and delivery are necessarily expensive, but that effort is certainly required to reach a level where "excellence" is the right way to describe the outcome. "The key, ultimately, is to capture and retain the attention of students, so they can truly learn and improve their performance. We believe that by creating engagement in learning we also create engagement on the part of our people with the entire company. And that translates into additional return on learning: increasing the retention rate of your best employees."

Getting engaged

Most organizations today have a challenge on their hands when it comes to creating an engaged workforce—people who are committed to the organization's goals and motivated and inspired in the quest to meet them. Difficult economic times tend to do that: companies in crisis mode focus more on the crisis than on the people working to overcome it. Yet when the storm passes and organizations turn to ask employees, "How are you doing?" they may not like the answer. A 2004 Gallup Q12 survey of more than 3 million employees found that 71 percent describe themselves as disengaged or actively disengaged from their work—the fourth straight year of decline in this area. And a recent Accenture survey of more than 500 full-time middle managers from a number of US companies found that one in five is either currently looking or plans to look for another job. One crisis leads to another.

Getting a workforce engaged can pay off. Accenture research has shown that the more engaged the workforce, the more innovative, productive and profitable the company. No wonder a recent survey of 71 executives reveals that business leaders consider employee engagement to be critically important to the competitive success of their companies.[3]

In another research study conducted to determine the specific practices that make the most difference to workers' sense of engagement, Accenture analyzed employee engagement and human capital process data from implementations of the Accenture Human Capital Development Framework with 26 organizations. This framework is a diagnostic and analytic tool that draws on best practices and Accenture experience in the fields of human resource development, learning and knowledge management, and workforce productivity, along with state-of-the-art measurement techniques. The framework is unique in that it helps organizations do more than look at levels of spending to get a sense of their human capital development strengths. It draws on business data, as well as survey and interview data, to enable a more rigorous and reliable assessment of the true *effectiveness* of each human capital process and capability. (See Chapter 9 for more about the framework.)

Based on our analysis, we were able to make the correlation between organizations that invest intelligently in people processes and programs, and the engagement levels of their workforces. We performed statistical analyses to determine the specific activities or attributes within each process that account for the most variation in employee engagement.

Here are our top 10 recommendations for increasing the engagement of a workforce:

1. Ensure that recognition and rewards are clearly and consistently tied to job performance and overall business results.
2. Ensure that human resources systems provide employees with the data they need to perform their work in a timely, accurate and consistent manner.
3. Provide the learning opportunities needed for employees to excel at their current jobs and to grow into new ones.
4. Provide employees with the means to find the knowledge and resources they need to perform optimally.
5. Provide frequent, direct performance appraisals.
6. Create a physical workplace environment conducive to high performance.
7. Communicate details about major organizational changes, and initiate programs to reduce the negative impact of such changes on morale and productivity.
8. Provide frequent and personalized attention to employees' career development and planning.
9. Ensure that HR programs and policies are consistent and fair for all employees.
10. Recruit from a pool of people most likely to be engaged with the organization's mission.

Four types of experiences that shape the return on learning

The team's further refinement of the phenomenal learning idea resulted in the creation of a four-part model, as seen in Figure 1.

Delivering phenomenal learning involves a focus on four interrelated experiences: learning, networking, enculturation and the "guest experience" itself.

Learning experience

The learning experience is the most important thing—though not the only thing—to get right. Creating a phenomenal learning ex-

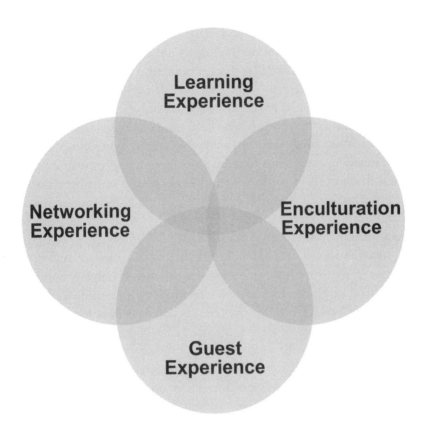

Figure 1. The Accenture Phenomenal Learning Model

perience begins with shifting from the traditional concentration on learning-program content, toward the performance outcomes the learning is intended to produce. Such an emphasis is obvious to most people when they think of particularly critical jobs, such as airline pilots. What everyone wants when it comes to pilot training is an outcome: a safe take-off, journey and landing. Scores on written tests might be important in assessing piloting skills, but good performance in a flight simulator would be even more important.

Many roles in today's organizations—especially customer-facing roles—can be thought of in a similar way. In customer service, for example, agents who have in-depth knowledge of the product catalog should be prized, to be certain—but perhaps not as much as those who are adept at interacting with customers in way that creates high levels of satisfaction and loyalty. Ideally, one would wish to deal with a personable agent who also knows a lot. But lacking that, most people would choose the positive interaction with an agent who cares about their needs over an extremely knowledgeable but otherwise cranky agent. So an effective learning experience for a customer service agent would keep that distinction in mind, and would shape the learning around the performance outcome—positive customer interactions embodying a branded customer experience—instead of a more narrow focus just on product knowledge.

A number of techniques help to strengthen the connection between the learning experience and the work or performance outcome. Pre-work, for example—readings or electronic learning done as a prerequisite for the course—can help people make the transition from their jobs to the learning experience in the classroom. Similarly, follow-up training or "post-requisites" can help employees move back from the classroom environment to the real world. It's vital not to simply dump a lot of content into pre-work or follow-up work just to give designers and leadership the satisfaction of being able to say that the content has been covered.

Phenomenal learning is not "one size fits all." It considers the make-up of the audience for the course, and it uses learning techniques and strategies that work well for that audience. Storytelling and the use of personal narratives—especially a consistent, clear storyline that runs through the entire experience—is one important element of courses delivered to Accenture employees. The sharing of stories—especially of challenges that were faced and overcome—helps to teach both content and character. An educational philosophy that goes back to ancient Greece and Aristotle tells us that people learn character and virtue-oriented behavior largely by imitation. An executive leading a class is, therefore, both a teacher and a model for the behavior of the students in the class. Opportunities for personal coaching and mentoring need to be designed into the overall course plan whenever possible.

An effective learning experience in corporate education also engages students by drawing them into a difficult problem or issue, especially one that counters or challenges their existing mental models. Often called "goal-based learning," such a technique can draw participants together to meet a given challenge, and it also sets a finite goal within the course chronology for closing off discussion of one topic and moving onto another. The best teachers and leaders in corporate education also know how to build reflective time into a class. After presentations about the challenge or issue, time should then be allotted for discussion and assimilation of content, so the experience can be refracted through the minds of the students.

This reflective time also is important for ongoing improvement of the course material. The feedback and reflections from students can serve as an impetus for changes to the course material and teaching approach, and for specific ideas about course content. So the best corporate education programs have a way of capturing this feedback and cycling it back as continuous improvements are made to the class.

Networking experience

The focus on networking during the learning experience—building relationships among students and faculty—is an example of how members of Vanthournout's team themselves embodied the principle of adapting and continuously improving their training offerings. Vanthournout recalls, "Our course evaluations from students were regularly telling us that the value of the St. Charles experience resided not only in the learning of content, but also in the relationship building and networking with peers from all over the world. So in subsequent iterations of classes we made sure to build downtime and free time into most days to enable those interactions to happen."

This commitment to networking also provided a mechanism to reinforce the Accenture core value of "one global network." Part of Accenture's success in the marketplace is due to the fact that its people act as a single, networked company and not as an international company with offices in 48 countries. Early on in the definition of the new learning curriculum, the steering committee determined that it was important that key learning events during an Accenture career be attended by global audiences. As employees are brought together for these classroom events, typically in the St. Charles training center, individuals have the opportunity to build relationships with peers from around the globe, and these relationships can then be leveraged to deliver better service to clients.

Part of the networking experience relates to the distinctive character of the learning experience as it is designed. That is, a pedagogy where small groups or teams work together to meet a goal or solve a challenging problem is, by its very nature, a relationship-building exercise. It also simulates the actual work environment of an Accenture professional, and asks students to engage in the give-and-take of working with peers for a common cause. The courses taken by new hires and younger professionals at Accenture often create bonds that last throughout the careers of those in the class. Many of the Accenture senior executives now approaching retirement could probably name a large percentage of the people who were in their "start group," especially those who remained at Accenture throughout their careers.

Opportunities for free-form discussion during a course are also network-building exercises, and opportunities for social interaction—above and beyond the business-focused interaction—are more than just optional or "nice to have" aspects of the experience. The personal coaching aspect of the class by an executive instructor is a way to build relationships between students and faculty, and also another way that behavior modeling takes place.

Finally, one can understand all people within a company as actually comprising many small networks. So an interaction among 20 or 30 students is in fact an interaction among networks, not just individuals. It's important to bear in mind that the networking experience extends beyond those in the immediate classroom environment. Students also need to be familiarized with those outside the immediate learning experience who can serve as expert counsel for particular content areas. Today's knowledge-sharing technologies can help here. Accenture, for example, has an internal database—experts.accenture.com—organized by content areas, in which professionals are grouped according to their areas of expertise and client experiences so they can serve as resources for anyone in the global organization.

Enculturation experience

As an "experience," and not just a means to pour content into people's heads, learning is an opportunity to participate in the culture of the entire company and to understand what it means to be a part of the whole. At Accenture, the classroom experience in St. Charles becomes part of the cultural fabric of the company. There are occasions in every class where the core values of the company can be reinforced and highlighted, where the company's heritage can be discussed and where Accenture's global culture and diversity can be embraced. Because many client projects at Accenture will involve a mix of people from around the world, it is vital for people from different nations and cultures to interact with each other in the classroom. There are innumerable presumptions and ways of looking at the world that are often unique to a particular culture, and all employees need to understand how their presumptions are not necessarily universal but are by-products of their education and culture.

Corporate education can also bring people into the culture of the company by tying the content of a course—even down to particular tasks and actions—to the larger business strategy of the company. This can help participants to realize that they are not simply engaging in rote classroom work, but activities vital to the company's long-term success. Courses foster a sense of community and belonging by letting participants know that they are essential parts of something larger that is happening around them.

It's also important to remember that every training or learning activity—all assignments, materials and teaching methods—are, in fact, a reflection of the entire organization. Just as every customer service agent is representing the brand of the entire company during a customer interaction, so every executive faculty member and every course offering is representing the company brand during a class, whether it is classroom-based or electronically delivered. There is an "Accenture way"—a distinctive corporate identity—and one of the things that Vanthournout's team did was to build upon the company's marketing and advertising strategy that has defined a distinctive Accenture brand, and then bring that identity and "feel" into the course materials. In addition, at the more detailed course level, the ways in which the training proceeds—particularly with goal-based learning—need to reflect the actual processes and methods used in client work.

To this end, it's important to select faculty with this modeling in mind. Executives should embody the organizational culture—they should be people who are passionate about their work and who are advocates for the distinctive quality of the company. Henry David Thoreau once wrote that when two people are interacting, *who* they are often speaks so loudly that they cannot hear *what* each other is saying. This is occasionally a burden, but it is a lesson that true leaders must bear in mind. Who they are, the character they represent, is at least as important as what they are teaching.

As noted, the presence of executives in Accenture's classrooms is itself a strong statement about the core values of the company. It says that these executives care about their stewardship responsibilities—their duty to pass on to their younger colleagues the same benefits they received as younger professionals. It's what Accenture refers to as "leaders teaching leaders"—part of the leadership mantra at Accenture.

Are all executives by nature good instructors? One could only wish this were so. But their experience and their presence are vital. To help these executives get up to speed quickly on the course material they will present, Accenture supports them with "learning coaches" who help them assimilate the material during preparation, and who also then provide feedback to the faculty on their presentations and interactions with the participants. These coaches are support personnel with deep communication and coaching skills, as well as deep knowledge of the course material. They ensure that the executives get as much out of the experience as the students.

Why? Because the elements of learning, culture and networking are being experienced by the faculty, too, and not just the students. Vanthournout notes, "There is never an occasion when an executive serving as faculty does not find himself or herself enriched by the teaching experience. Educational psychologists have always known that the best learning experiences—the ones that result in the most effective retention of knowledge—come from teaching the material. In addition, our executives inevitably come away from their time in St. Charles even more hopeful about the future of the company, because they have just spent several days interacting with some very smart and talented people. In other words, the learning and enculturation works on the executives' behalf, too. In fact, I secretly suspect many of them go back home with the sense that they had better stay on their toes, because they've seen that the up-and-coming generation already knows a lot and has the spirit and energy to succeed. That's one of the best things about our meritocracy; it energizes people at every level."

Jill Smart echoes this sense that "leaders teaching leaders" is good for both sides of the equation. "Almost every time one of our senior executives comes to St. Charles to teach, I get a follow-up note from him or her telling me how valuable an experience it was. I hear from them a great sense of pride that they were able to help people at an early stage of their careers, just as the executives themselves were helped when they were younger."

Guest experience

Finally, again, there is the "guest" experience itself—surprising and delighting learners by the quality, engagement and "festive" nature of the time in the classroom. Making that happen involves, in part, applying some of the best practices from the field of customer service to the learning environment—to learners and faculty alike.

Everyone with whom the guests have contact is friendly and willing to help. Registration processes are carefully planned to minimize any hassles; if the course involves a hotel stay at the St. Charles campus, the check-in process is fast and easy. The classrooms are well-designed for effective learning; technology used should work flawlessly; all materials are professionally written and designed, with strong graphic and media elements that connote the excellence and professionalism of the company, and that reinforce the company's brand. All communications related to the course are professionally designed and executed (and kept to a minimum in this age of e-mail glut). Manual processes are automated, whenever possible, to minimize any administrative burden on participants and faculty. Opportunities for fun and relaxation are built into the learning experience, too, and periodic breaks in the class are provided so guests can recharge, refresh and reconnect with their lives back home.

Making all training phenomenal

This discussion certainly does not exhaust the concept of phenomenal learning. Successfully executing learning programs based on the experience or phenomena surrounding learning delivery is not something that necessarily can be achieved by following a checklist. Delivering phenomenal learning is really a mindset more than anything. As organizations think about their learning assets and how to incorporate some of the principles of phenomenal learning, they should ask themselves questions such as:

- Am I considering every aspect of the training experience—learning, networking, enculturation and guest experience?
- Am I focused on the entire experience, from first contact to last contact?

- What might I do, above and beyond the course materials, to surprise and delight my participants?

As Olson concludes, "Although it may be an overused phrase now, phenomenal learning was truly the 'secret sauce' for many of the positive outcomes we have accomplished with the learning transformation initiative at Accenture. Phenomenal learning was how all the good planning and design came to life. It's how the 'thinking' and the 'doing' all came together to produce phenomenal results."

Phenomenal electronic learning

Creating and delivering phenomenal learning goes beyond the classroom experience. Here are some essential components of phenomenal electronic learning, as well:

Computer-based training (CBT)

- **Matching delivery mechanism to need.** CBT is most appropriate when the content is best learned, and the performance outcomes are best practiced, individually. CBT is also the right delivery vehicle when messages need to be consistent and when the content is reasonably stable. It should also be considered when the knowledge and experience of a small number of experienced personnel need to be spread among a large number of learners.
- **Access, usability and quality.** There is a "guest experience" in electronic learning, too. Just as classroom learning seeks to make registration and check-in as hassle-free as possible, so companies must make it easy to find and then navigate through the learning content in an electronic environment. If the course isn't easy to get to and to use, and if it isn't free of technical defects, then all the content and design may be for naught. The quality of the writing and graphics is an important part of delivering a branded experience—an experience that

speaks for and represents the culture of the company. Poorly written material in terms of substance, structure, grammar or punctuation can distract learners and can even lower the bar for an individual's own performance. ("If the learning designers didn't care," an employee may say, "why should I?")

- **Information structure and design.** Delivering an effective experience in electronic learning means, in part, personalizing the experience—or, at least, allowing learners to personalize it themselves. That is, participants should be able to select relevant content and opt out of content with which they are already familiar. They should not be forced onto a linear path that allows no deviation (unless such a path is dictated by content such as compliance or ethics training). Through the choice of appropriate media—graphics, video, tables and so forth—the design of the content should keep the learning experience in mind and help the learner maintain interest. Activities that allow learners to practice or apply learning content should occur at the right intervals, appropriate to the type of content, when reinforcement and practice are logically called for. Activities should be designed around how learners should apply the information just presented. As with classroom training, learners have the best experience when the focus is on performance outcomes or behaviors that need to result, not just the content they need to read or hear.

Virtual seminars

- **The right use of seminars.** A virtual seminar is best used when the goal of the learning experience is primarily disseminating information rather than building skills. At Accenture, for example, these seminars (also called "webinars") are often planned when new services or offerings are available to clients, and/or when experiences on a project need to be shared with other professionals doing similar work. A virtual seminar is also an ideal delivery vehicle when the content is new or constantly changing, and when the desire or need is to maximize the impact of a relatively small number of experts.

- **Interaction and eliminating distractions.** Passivity and distraction are the enemies of virtual learning. It is important to build audience interaction into the design, as well as opportunities for learners to ask questions of presenters during the seminar. At the same time, leaders may need to explicitly ask participants to abide by an honor code of not engaging in other work during the virtual seminar. Today, people are bombarded with mobile phone calls, pages, instant messages and e-mail. No matter what individuals may think about their ability to multitask, in fact the learning experience is compromised by these distractions (imagine trying to learn in a classroom while two or three people are simultaneously talking). If the learning experience is compromised, this also means that, from a financial perspective, the return on learning is being compromised. Thus, demanding that learners focus on the learning experience at hand is more than a personal responsibility; it is a corporate one.

- **Registration and technology issues.** As with CBT, a focus on the "guest" experience means in part that the technology works. This is sometimes a challenge, with people working from many locations and using many kinds of computers. Such issues must be anticipated and dealt with long before the day of the seminar. The guest experience also means that all registration processes, learning support and help desk support must be highly professional in nature.

Virtual workshops

- **The use of workshops.** Organizations are using more virtual workshops as collaboration and distance learning technologies become more sophisticated. Yet virtual learning can be a challenge, too, as the virtual environment often taxes the limits of a person's ability to maintain focus. These workshops become a good option when the learning experience is such that only a couple days of live interaction is necessary, making classroom events impractical or not cost-effective.

- **Pacing.** Pacing and planning are vital to the success of a workshop. If there is content for approximately two business days of training, it is best to stretch the event over four days rather than try to squeeze it into two. There is a reason why university seminars last only three hours or so; that is about the reasonable limit of the human attention span. The goal, again, is to deliver an effective learning experience, not just to be able to check a box that says the content has been covered. Variety is important. Offer a mix of individual activity and group discussion. Provide opportunities for networking and fun, and build in frequent breaks. Participants should not be forced into long stretches of time in the virtual environment.

- Effective learning programs are not just about the content or information to be covered and mastered; they also are about the entire *experience* surrounding learning and the delivery of a course.
- Employees taking a learning program are experiencing the quality of their company's brand: what it means to work for that company, the values a company stands for and the type of culture that binds together its people.
- Today, many of the most successful company brands are built on the delivery of differentiated customer experiences. Similarly, companies that leverage learning for business results must focus on the learning experience.
- "Phenomenal" learning must address the whole learning experience, with a focus on engaging learners in a way that creates the desired behaviors and also strengthens the bond between employees and the company.
- Successful learning executives ask, "What else can we do to create a learning experience that has the potential to change someone's career or even change someone's life?" High-performance learning organizations strive to touch an employee's entire experience with the company through learning.
- Phenomenal learning means creating a surprising and delighting level of excellence in every aspect of the learning experience. That means designing the experience so it engages both the intellect and the emotions.
- Effective learning experiences must be built on heavy participation from managers and executives as faculty.
- Creating engagement in learning can also create engagement on the part of employees with the entire company.
- Effective learning requires moving away from the traditional concentration on content and toward achieving the desired performance outcomes.
- Phenomenal learning is not "one size fits all." It considers the make up of the learning population or audience for the

course, and it uses learning techniques and strategies that work well for that particular audience.

- Networking—building relationships among students and faculty—is a vital part of effective corporate education.
- Learning is an opportunity to participate in the culture of the entire company and to understand what it means to be a part of the whole.

Notes

1. B. Joseph Pine II and James H. Gilmore, *The Experience Economy* (Cambridge, MA: Harvard Business School Press, 1999), page 2.

2. Pine and Gilmore, page 5.

3. The survey was administered as part of implementations of the Accenture Human Capital Development Framework in 26 organizations in 2003/2004.

▶ *Six*

Running Learning Like a Business

For all the innovation and unique approaches at the heart of Accenture's evolving capabilities and strategies in its learning programs, one aspect of the challenge was not unique: the pressure to deliver more for less, and the drive to squeeze out costs and improve operating efficiency while still delivering measurable value to the business. In 1999 and 2000, Accenture had spent more than $700 million a year to deliver learning programs to its employees. These were high-value, award-winning programs. But 70 percent of them were being delivered in classrooms—on the campus in St. Charles, and in a number of other countries as well. Learning was a very big, very noticeable budget line item. According to Jill Smart, "It was inevitable that such a large number—the largest non-payroll item in our operating budget—would come under management scrutiny, especially as the world economy at that time began to flounder."

In fact, that kind of scrutiny is now the name of the game in almost every industry. According to an Accenture Learning survey of 285 chief learning officers and other learning executives in a variety of industries, many new demands are being placed on the learning function today. The most pressing demands involve aligning learning with the business and measuring the impact of learning on overall business results. The reason: senior management expectations have changed. The "cost center" mentality about learning is a thing of the past. Learning organizations now must deliver business value and prove the business impact of learning investments.

The Accenture Learning research highlights the fact that senior management increasingly measures the performance of learning executives in terms of how well they manage the business side of learning, and how well they meet defined business outcomes. For example, the top three performance criteria by which executives surveyed were measured are "ability to prove business impact of learning and development programs" (73 percent), "managing budget to business plan" (69 percent) and "ability of the learning department to increase access to learning while reducing costs" (57 percent). To meet these expectations, learning professionals increasingly are seeking new kinds of competencies. Chief learning officers today should be as concerned with business acumen and strategic planning as with the details of learning design and delivery. Their bosses know that if a company is not "running learning like a business," it is likely to find itself falling behind in the marketplace.

At Accenture, operational excellence clearly was a mandate for the learning function. As Don Vanthournout recalls, "Our executive leadership didn't say to us, 'Here's an unlimited budget, go create great learning.' In effect, they said, 'We need you to give back about half of your budget. *Now* go create great learning.'"

The components of business-centric learning

Accenture's own experience—as a consultant in the learning area, as a provider of internal training and as a provider of learning-related outsourcing services—had led to the conclusion that the capability to run learning like a business requires mastery in three different areas:

1. Plotting and measuring a course toward upside value creation—determining the particular value objectives (using financial measures of such things as shareholder value, book or market value, employee and

customer value, etc.) most closely linked to the learning investments.

2. Governance and sponsorship—putting in place the governance structures and decision-making mechanisms that enable the learning organization to understand the business well enough to direct the learning outcomes that affect business results, and then to manage relationships with key decision makers, making sure that learning is included in the management agenda from a planning and business management perspective.

3. Efficiency planning and management—using the best cost management techniques to drive business results with the most efficient use of resources.

The Accenture team already had in place the first two components of this overall mastery. Its ROI study had established—with a rigor that placed it almost beyond dispute—that learning at Accenture delivered an annual net benefit of more than $25,000 per person for the company (see Chapter 3). Also, the team had assembled a governance body or executive steering committee, comprising the heads of its major internal organizations, to provide input, validate the strategic learning model and sponsor the effort to implement the model across the company (see Chapter 4). Indeed, these two components worked together: the ROI study had successfully energized the steering committee about the potential for upside value creation from Accenture's learning programs. Management was favorably disposed toward the learning transformation initiative. At the same time, the Accenture team had not sacrificed the quality of the learning experiences, either in the classroom or with technology-delivered learning.

So, the vision and goals were right, the value to be produced was clear, the structure for management and oversight was sound, the learning programs themselves were high-quality and oriented toward supporting the necessary behaviors and capabilities to support employees at each stage of their careers. But unless the team could put operational strategies, mechanisms and technologies in place to deliver predictably and cost-effectively, even the best strategies and programs would not be enough to ensure success, and management would not be able to continue its strong sponsorship and support.

However favorably disposed management was toward the learning transformation program, many demands were being placed on budgets during what was, at the time, an extraordinarily difficult time in the world economy. As Jill Smart puts it, "Most of our senior executives had grown up as professionals within Accenture and had fond memories of their own days at the central campus in St. Charles. Years ago, as new recruits, they had spent their first three weeks as employees there, and few ever forgot the experience. So they already were favorably disposed, in the abstract, toward reinvigorating global learning at Accenture. But however misty their eyes became when recalling their own experiences as younger students, they were now business operators with a need to watch and justify every penny spent according to business value created." In other words, getting the operational aspects of learning design and delivery right was going to be essential for Vanthournout and his team.

Not the most glamorous work

Essential, yes, but not necessarily the most glamorous side of it, at least according to Andy White. White, who led the operational aspects of Accenture's learning transformation initiative and heads global operations for the capability development function, has been with the central training organization at Accenture longer than anyone else on the core team. In many respects, he has experienced the roller-coaster ride of the company's learning effort more than many others. It is White's job to make sure the company spends its money on training delivery wisely and maximizes the business impact of that expenditure, while delivering quality learning experiences that are worthy of Accenture's reputation.

"Running learning like a business for a major company," says White, "is partly about finding the right balance: between a desire to make the learning experiences rich and, as we say, 'phenomenal,' and the necessity to deliver those experiences efficiently as well." It's also about applying good project and program management skills to learning—a business domain that has not always been managed with necessary rigor. "The former, legacy training group at Accenture was operating in a situation that I think a lot of companies still are in today," says White. "It had come to view itself primarily in a service delivery role, rather than in a role central to the business—one that needs to be managed with the rigor *of* a business. We needed a learning organization that could execute within a budget, make tough decisions about what we can afford and not afford to do, delivering training timed to meet a business need. That's really what it means to run learning like a business."

Diagnosis

Vanthournout and team worked over the early months of the learning transformation program to create and refine a business case. That work began with a diagnosis of the company's current situation. Much of that part of the story has already been told in previous chapters. In addition, however, the team had to make several other key decisions to ensure that the operations of the learning function would become ingrained and systemic, and thus successful over the long term. Olson recalls that the team spent a great deal of time upfront determining the direction for several key operational decisions:

1. How to maximize the impact of different types of learning delivery mechanisms, such as e-learning, computer-based training (CBT), virtual training and classroom-based learning.
2. How to systemically make curricula decisions ensuring that the best choices could be made regarding delivery

mechanisms (again, e-learning, CBT or classroom) for specific types of performance outcomes and audiences.

3. How to specify the core or strategic competencies of the learning function at Accenture.

4. How to outline the kinds of information that would be needed to run the learning business on an ongoing basis.

Once the Accenture team was clear on those questions, the remaining operational decisions began to fall into place.

Making the learning delivery decisions

Budget pressures were being felt rather intensely by Vanthournout's learning team. Andy White recalls, "We were under a great deal of budget pressure, and that was a big impetus toward improving operations. But, in fact, a lot of that pressure was a self-inflicted wound. We had made it easy to cut our budgets, because we hadn't adequately made the case that we were delivering solid value—that is, that we were delivering learning experiences that were making an impact on people's capabilities and on the performance of the business. In late 2001, the tragedy of the September 11 terrorist attacks and the curtailment of travel made it look like these were the reasons for the decline in training days at the St. Charles campus: from 270,000 to 60,000 in just one year. But, really, behind it all was the fact that we had lost our crown jewels—our distinctive and effective approaches to core training and our other learning programs."

As discussed earlier, central training at Accenture had become fractured and factionalized to support a business model that put more power in the hands of the individual industry groups and capability groups at Accenture. "The technology people wanted their own learning curriculum, the strategy people wanted theirs and the change management leadership wanted their needs attended to," says White. "At the time, there seemed to be good business reasons for what was happening. But, in fact, that approach had a number of unintended consequences. Our curriculum had become hard to understand, and communicating its value was difficult. We had undercut the power of our learning offerings to support a common culture. And this had hurt our ability to deliver learning efficiently. We were using classroom learning as our default delivery approach without thinking carefully enough about whether it was the right delivery mechanism for the learning need. That meant we were spending more and more for less and less."

The right learning experience for the right business need

Given the heightened attention paid to e-learning in the press in recent years, it's worthwhile to look at the hard numbers in order to see the extent to which technology is altering traditional methods of enterprise learning. Overall, although the specific numbers can vary from study to study, roughly two-thirds of all corporate learning experiences occur in a classroom. And a recent Accenture Learning survey (see figure) has found that, even by 2008, learning executives on average expect 40 percent of learning still to be classroom-based and instructor-led.

By the year 2008, what percentage of your total course offerings will be delivered using the following delivery methods?

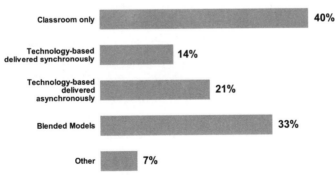

Source: Accenture Learning Research

So, very few learning experts expect—or even want—face-to-face learning programs to go away. Obviously, in most cases e-learning creates cost savings compared with classroom-based learning, simply by removing travel and housing costs from the equation. But a lower investment figure is no bargain if it delivers a sub-optimal learning experience that has little to no impact on performance. Many companies today brag about the thousands of e-learning titles in their catalogs. And because they compile their financial data by spreading their total investment across all the titles, their costs can seem dramatically low. But look closer into how many titles actually are being used and the impact they are having on employee performance, and the cost analysis is quite different indeed.

The more important need in enterprise learning is to increase the sophistication with which organizations plan the right mix or blend of learning experiences, according to what delivery method is most appropriate to the performance need and business goal. "Blended" learning is the goal: a learning delivery program that mixes or blends classroom experiences with self-study electronic learning and interactive virtual classrooms.

Operational improvements, therefore, had to be founded on a more coherent curriculum. The development of that curriculum, discussed in Chapter 2, had resulted in an overall learning strategy that combined two approaches. First, a centralized and primarily classroom-based approach—leveraging the St. Charles training campus—focused on building an essential set of common and core skills, such as leadership, communications and relationship building. Second, a more specialized set of capabilities—deep industry skills and advanced knowledge in specialty areas like CRM, financial management and supply chain management—would be designed and delivered as a combination of classroom-based and technology-based offerings.

In both classroom-based and technology-based learning, Vanthournout's team found much to improve in the way of operations. Although the importance of returning to common class-room learning experiences at the St. Charles campus was universally affirmed among Accenture leadership, there was a right way to do that—and several wrong ways. "We were going 'back to the future' with our common curriculum," says Vanthournout, "but of course we couldn't return to the business environment of the 1980s and 1990s. We could not return to the 'mass production' system where the content of training and learning was predictable and fairly limited in its range and number of areas to be covered, and where large volumes of participants with similar learning needs came together in primarily a classroom setting."

In that more stable business environment, and in a headier economic environment, it had been easier to approach Accenture's common curriculum in the 1990s with the attitude of, "Let's give everyone the same courses and curriculum, in case they need it." But that approach can be tremendously wasteful. In reality, there is a fairly predictable set of employees for whom certain kinds of learning courses are not needed. It's as if one gave winter coats to all employees, whether they lived in Norway or Nigeria. Borrowing from the language of manufacturing, the Accenture team concluded that the company needed to transform its education approach from a system of mass production to a system of custom, just-in-time production that responds to the changing needs of its people and the marketplace. The shift would be from a supplier-centric model to a consumer-centric model that would support customized skills-building at the point-of-need, focused always on the changing needs of the business. As Vanthournout notes, "Our goal was a more nimble implementation approach that would prioritize our learning investments to first address the skill gaps with the largest business impact, and then allow us to measure our progress."

Bringing learning content and delivery back into alignment with the business also was a huge priority. Accenture's clients had different attitudes in 2001 than they may have had in 1991 or 1981. Greater client sophistication and heightened competition meant more pressure on newer Accenture professionals to perform at higher levels of competence more quickly. As with many companies with roots in professional services, Accenture had relied on an apprenticeship model, where a great deal of learning occurred on the job. But with clients expecting more expert practitioners on site, Accenture had to stay ahead of these expectations.

A primarily classroom-centric model also had become wasteful in terms of the life span of the learning content. For many of the experienced instructional designers at Accenture, those who had hit their stride in the late 1980s and early 1990s, the life span of a learning asset had been measured in years. At the dawn of the 21st century, a learning designer's greatest fear was that classroom materials would be out-of-date as soon as they were delivered to the classroom. An investment of, say, $1 million in a classroom experience that would remain relevant for two years or more could be supported, and had been supported for years at Accenture. But that same investment for an experience that would be out of date in six months was pretty hard to justify. In addition, as Andy White notes, "It's in exactly those volatile content areas where the business opportunities are often greatest and most strategically desirable. So both our executives and our professionals, for somewhat different reasons, were coming to expect highly relevant, immediate educational support in content areas that are subject to sometimes unpredictable change."

The training and learning situation was not entirely bleak, of course. The internal capability development group already had put in place a leading-edge learning management system and technology infrastructure for virtual learning, called "myLearning" (more on this in the next chapter). That centralized learning infrastructure already was giving Accenture the means to communicate and explain curricula to its people; deliver e-learning, computer-based training and virtual seminars; and then to track the results centrally. This infrastructure, in fact, was vital to mitigating (as much as possible) the effects on Accenture's learning programs in late 2001 and early 2002, following the September 11, 2001, terrorist attacks in New York and Washington. Although many learning events were in other cases cancelled, materials could be placed in myLearning, virtual courses could be conducted and training could continue, at least in some form.

Even in the technology area, however, Vanthournout's team knew that times had changed and that Accenture's e-learning design and delivery environment had to keep up. As White says, "Just as with our classroom learning, we had a lot of award-winning courses that were no longer appropriate to the needs of our employees and the way they were really working out in the field with clients. You can't take a classroom mentality—where you have a captive audience on the St. Charles campus for more than 40 hours a week—and move that over to CBT or e-learning. No one has 40 hours to sit in front of a computer and take an e-learning course. We had to get more focused in the way we delivered electronic learning, and then we needed to design and deliver experiences more appropriate to the working lives of our employees."

To achieve and maintain the maximum benefits of both classroom and virtual/electronic learning, the Accenture team was guided by a learning delivery and decision-making model that assigned the appropriate delivery method according to two factors: the extent to which participants need to interact with content in order to master it, and the level of interactivity they need with fellow participants to absorb and apply the content. (See Figure 1.)

Using this model, one can see that if, for example, there is a need for high interaction with both content and people—upper right of the model—a global classroom experience would be the most appropriate delivery mode. If, on the other hand, high interaction with content is needed, but interaction with people is not—upper left of the model—then an electronic experience such as multimedia performance simulation is likely to be the most effective and most cost-efficient delivery vehicle. It was this model that guided the Accenture team toward balancing two critical aspects of its learning reinvention program: the need to return Accenture, to a degree, to the days of face-to-face learning events

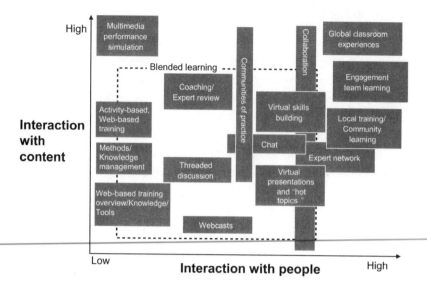

Figure 1. The Accenture Model for Learning Delivery and Decision Making.

at a common site, in pursuit of sustained cultural assimilation, while also using less expensive delivery methods when it made the most sense.

As in any organization, cost and quality must constantly be balanced. Accenture was able to balance these demands because of the people in the solution planner roles—those who were in charge of Business Interlock, ensuring that the learning offerings were locked onto the most important business needs of the company. The solution planner/Business Interlock roles brought Accenture's vision for learning to life: planning the curricula, managing the sponsorship of the curricula and ensuring the curricula were doable within the cost constraints. Solution planners were charged with assessing the curricula needs and planning the appropriate delivery vehicles to meet those needs.

By applying the Accenture Model for Learning Delivery and Decision Making to the curricula, solution planners can work to ensure that classroom-based delivery is only used when achieving the maximum value of the learning experience actually requires bringing people physically together. This more nuanced approach to matching learning need with the appropriate delivery vehicle allows a company to leverage lower-cost, non-classroom delivery vehicles when appropriate. In too many cases, curriculum and course sponsors automatically assume that the classroom is the best delivery vehicle, so the solution planner must manage the change process to ensure that sponsors apply the decision-making model as well. As Kurt Olson notes, "Solution planners are, first and foremost, business people. They make critical business decisions on a daily basis and apply discipline to the learning planning process. They make the curricula phenomenal as well as affordable for Accenture."

Toward more effective cost management for the learning function

In Accenture's experience, when it comes to large-scale training delivery, three drivers account for about 80 percent of the variability around the proper leverage of resources.

1. Migration to e-learning

Cost savings from e-learning are now well documented, and they manifest themselves in a number of ways. The first is a decrease in direct costs: lower program tuitions as well as the reduction or elimination of items such as facilities and travel costs, instructor fees and a great percentage of publishing and printing costs. Accenture has developed for its clients extremely accurate "gearing ratios" for cost savings from e-learning. That is, Accenture can spell out how companies will realize impressive reductions in cost per student day of training, for certain percentage increases in migration of instructor-led training to e-learning, accompanied by corresponding increases in e-learning investments.

For most companies, the relative percentage of student days delivered via technology-enabled learning is still far from optimal. This phenomenon is particularly true in some industries, such as financial services, retail and health care, where many of the right elements are in place to justify large-scale migration to e-learning. The combination of large, highly distributed workforces, a high degree of technical and product knowledge content and high turnover is a likely recipe for accelerated and large scale e-learning initiatives. But even in less likely situations, such as in manufacturing and resources companies, examples exist of aggressive e-learning programs. Overall, dramatic breakthroughs in cost leverage can result from challenging traditional assumptions of user acceptance, technical barriers and near-term investments.

Another aspect of cost savings derived from e-learning lies in the so-called "opportunity costs." That is, most companies can easily quantify the cost of lost productivity involved in employee travel to reach a training event or when employees simply need time away from their jobs. In this latter case, one accepted industry standard is that employees can get as much out of a one-hour e-learning experience as from a two-hour instructor-led course. Less time away from the job means more productivity on the job.

When some companies calculate return on investment, however, their estimates of "productivity gains" stemming from e-learning are controversial. Finance managers often are reluctant to count such "soft dollar" savings as tangible benefits—yet, in some industries, these savings are extremely tangible. Defense industries, for example, are highly sensitive to labor rate calculations. For them, small savings in labor time, calculated over many workers, provide a significant value to either margin or cost competitiveness. In other industries, while such labor gains are not used to justify investments, they are still estimated and counted "below the line." Whether factored into business cases or not, these productivity gains certainly are real to employees and their managers.

2. More effective vendor management

In enterprise training today, it's not unusual for vendors to account for as much as 30 to 50 percent of the total cost of the solution. As a result, procurement and vendor management become big opportunities for cost reduction. The problem, though, is that too often a highly disaggregated (sometimes used as a polite term for "disorganized") training function leads to a great deal of waste, redundancy and lost opportunities for cost savings. An audit of spending by one major company found that it had seven different contracts with one vendor. By altering this arrangement to a single global contract, the company cut costs associated with that vendor by 50 percent.

Vendor consolidation presents another opportunity for savings. In most companies, some 10 percent of their vendors provide approximately half of their training programs. Clearly, such companies need to target their vendor discounting activities. But what about that other 90 percent of the vendors who provide the other half of the programs? That's where consolidation (followed by discounting) can again yield impressive savings. The value of such consolidation goes beyond cost: by decreasing the number of suppliers, companies can build stronger relationships with a smaller number of organizations, increasing the capacity of both sides to work together creatively.

Far from being a threat to training vendors, such partnerships offer great value both to them and the companies they serve. In leading companies, such arrangements have led to creative pricing and "risk-sharing" arrangements, which align the economic interests of both parties toward achieving performance goals. They also enable significant movement from "fixed" to "variable" costs, by shifting overhead and infrastructure costs to vendors, who can spread those costs over a much larger base. Finally, properly structured, these partnerships enable nimbleness and speed, by streamlining the typical laborious procurement process under a master servicing agreement.

Another consequence of decentralized training is enormous redundancy in course design and development. Some companies have as many as 100 different training and development groups, each providing non-strategic and non-proprietary programs. Accenture has seen clients, for example, that offer up to seven different ways of teaching negotiating skills. Are these courses in sync? Not exactly. Clearly, situations such as these offer companies the opportunity to lower the cost of maintaining redundant and sometimes conflicting intellectual property. Companies with multiple versions of content also multiply their maintenance costs when they have to update that content. Consolidating learning design activities, therefore, can create more consistent learning experiences and increase a company's ability to maintain content at significantly lower cost.

The effort to standardize content is well worth the effort. The industry has entered a new age of training content management, where content management tools and knowledge management technologies have converged to create powerful opportunities to rethink long-held beliefs about this area. Organizations now have the capacity for reuse, mass customization, personalization and wholesale change in printing and distribution. This is as much the case for instructor-led training content as for e-learning content. But taking advantage of such tools starts with a strategic approach to content management, and fundamental to that approach is recognizing such content as intellectual property—a valuable asset of the organization.

3. Process reengineering

One of the most important truths about learning management today is that updating technology without updating processes likely means a company is under-leveraging new technologies. But restructuring processes to refocus the roles and capabilities of training staff, which in turn provides greater strategic value to the organization, can be a critical source of both value and cost savings. In some companies, as much as 25 percent of all training staff time is spent in administration—getting people registered, dealing with cancellations, getting the training facility ready and so forth.

Through a variety of approaches, companies can address such process problems. They can update the organizational structures and processes used by the training group, or they can revise roles and responsibilities to maximize value for the investment. They can centralize certain functions to minimize the number of high-value professionals performing low-value tasks, or they can aggregate costly and time-consuming activities and then off-load them, perhaps through an outsourcing arrangement. They could also consider a shared services function for training design and delivery, which could eliminate the redundancies that result from having content developed in multiple locations. Additionally, increasing employee self-service could drastically reduce the cost of providing basic administrative functionality. No matter which approaches a company implements, the result can be tremendous cost savings.

Ironically, despite the proliferation of learning management systems, most learning organizations have not fundamentally changed the ways in which they deliver services. In far too many cases, such platforms essentially are used as back-end databases, rather than as enabling engines for dramatically enhanced workflows. It could be argued that, for most training organizations, governance lags behind technology. That is, companies have inserted new technologies into legacy governance structures, thereby diminishing their potential benefits. Such benefits, it should be noted, may not be found in training headcount reduction, but in transforming training staff workloads into more productive, higher-leverage activities.

The opportunity for more effective cost management

Accenture's experience suggests that for companies with a large training budget and with highly decentralized design and delivery assets, it is not unusual to be able to realize a 20 to 30 percent reduction in costs, while at the same time increasing impact through the greater business value created by the newly trained employees.

◆――――――――――――――――――――――――――◆

A more effective strategic sourcing strategy for learning design and delivery

Until the time of this learning transformation program, Accenture had, like most organizations, used its own dedicated team of employees to create proprietary learning content, support the execution of its classroom training program and maintain the learning infrastructure for the company. Now, to maximize cost efficiency, Accenture intended to develop and then follow a more sophisticated approach to strategic sourcing of learning design and delivery. Shared services and business process outsourcing (BPO) have become increasingly important strategies for companies across many industries and business functions, including learning. Accenture research has found, in fact, that in industries such as consumer and industrial products, learning is now second only to IT in terms of the prevalence of some sort of outsourcing arrangement. Leading IT market research firm IDC estimates the global learning BPO market to represent a $5 billion slice of annual corporate spending on external learning services. With a forecasted compound annual growth rate of more than 42 percent, learning BPO looks to be a $14.3 billion market by 2010.

The key question for Vanthournout and his team, however, was how to take a smarter and more nuanced approach to selecting which aspects of learning design and delivery would remain in-house, and which would be sourced to an external provider. Vanthournout developed an analytic approach (see Figure 2) that plotted various kinds of learning functions across a matrix of value. These functions can be:

- Transactional
- Enabling
- Knowledge-based
- Strategic

As the figure indicates, transactional and enabling functions such as registration and tracking tend to be lower-value processes that one wants to automate as much as possible because human intervention, internal or external, adds little value (and may even increase the risk of errors that lead to poor reporting).

Of greater value are strategic and transactional functions such as evaluation and reporting, and enabling and knowledge-based functions such as the administration and logistics aspects of training delivery. A large portion of training and content development also falls under this category. For these functions, com-

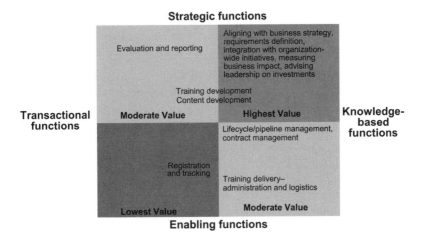

Figure 2. Accenture matrix for making strategic sourcing decisions about learning

panies do well to automate where possible, and then to pursue shared services and outsourcing models, not only for cost and efficiency reasons, but also to leverage the expertise of a provider whose core competency lies in these areas.

Finally, the highest-value learning functions are those that are knowledge-based and strategic. These kinds of activities include the methods put in place to keep learning aligned with business strategy (again, what Accenture calls "Business Interlock"), requirements definitions, integration with organization-wide initiatives, measuring business impact and advising leadership on where to invest for maximum business return. These are the functions organizations generally will want to continue to own, especially those organizations whose competitive advantage lies in their people, knowledge assets and intellectual property.

Beyond the Business Interlock function, Accenture retained several other key functions within its internal learning organization. Those functions included:

- Capability strategy—addressing Accenture's overall capability development strategy, curricula strategy and curricula architectures.

- Capability infrastructure—providing overall direction, requirements and content operations for the learning infrastructure, as well as managing the decision support/reporting capability for learning.
- Performance measurement—addressing the group's ongoing measurement strategy and ROI activities.
- Knowledge management—supporting the ongoing content management and knowledge-sharing functions at Accenture.

The decision to retain these functions was based primarily on business needs, and that is an important lesson for all organizations. "We retained the functions closest to our people," says Vanthournout, "Because, at Accenture, we are only as good as our people. They represent the company and its brand with our clients each and every day."

Outsourcing a function does not imply that it is not being operated well or that it is not "important." In fact, the learning functions that the Accenture team outsourced were, in many cases, world class. But the learning team at Accenture did not believe that those functions were core and/or strategic competencies of the internal learning function. Every company has to make its own decisions about what is core and what is not; that is the thinking behind the sourcing decision-making matrix.

For those learning functions for which the Accenture team decided to look for an outsourcing relationship, the company made an innovative move that has paid off handsomely in terms of both efficiency and effectiveness. Accenture created a separate business unit in the learning outsourcing marketspace, called "Accenture Learning," which consolidated its learning design and delivery resources within an organization that would serve clients as well as Accenture's own internal training organization. It was not just an internal bookkeeping move, but a way to drive revenue through advanced learning solutions and learning outsourcing. Indeed, Accenture Learning immediately made history with one of the first end-to-end enterprise learning outsourcing agreements ever established, with Avaya, a major communications and high-tech company.

From the perspective of Vanthournout's team, the creation of Accenture Learning meant that internal learning programs at Accenture would now be driven by the kind of efficiency that often results only from a supplier/customer relationship. As Kurt Olson notes, "When you're coordinating the work of different internal parties, the chain of command can be unclear at times, and objectives can conflict. With an outsourcing relationship, you get the best of both worlds. You get world-class talent supporting you, and yet it's a relationship that has 'pleasing the customer' at the heart of it, as well as driving costs lower because the provider can achieve economies of scale." Vanthournout adds, "Using an outsourcer for our training development and delivery activities allows my team to focus on the business issues and results we need to deliver, instead of spending time micromanaging headcount and project-level budget items. We know that Accenture Learning will provide the staff we need to get the job done. They own the issue of having the right number of skilled people to deliver the learning services."

Accenture Learning can provide those benefits in part because of a comprehensive delivery center network, leveraging experienced resources at the most cost-effective location. Five content development centers—two in the United States, two in Europe and one in Asia—provide round-the-clock development capabilities. To support its virtual classroom and Web-based delivery, it has five learning call centers offering 24/7 customer support in nine languages (Accenture Learning offers training in 143 countries).

As with the most effective learning outsourcing relationships, Accenture's relationship with Accenture Learning has gone far beyond simply driving down the cost of learning design and delivery (see box, "The right kind of learning outsourcing relationship"). The two entities have collaborated to deliver world-class experiences in classroom training, e-learning, virtual classrooms and decision support. As of this writing, Accenture and Accenture Learning work together to serve more than 126,000 Accenture employees annually through more than 160,000 classroom learning days and more than 1,000 virtual learning sessions. Nearly 8 million hours of training in total, including self-study and Web-based courses, are also supported through the myLearning system.

A comprehensive service level agreement between Vanthournout's group and Accenture Learning provides detailed definitions of the various service items and the levels and targets associated with those services. It also defines the responsibilities of each party, the interfaces between these parties, the methods of measuring service performance and the various reporting structures, in order to ensure that the relationship proceeds as smoothly as possible. Service level targets for budget, for example, specify zero variance or under budget; schedule targets are on or ahead of schedule. Weekly status reports help ensure these goals are met. From a technology standpoint, the monthly uptime average for the learning management system must be maintained at 98.5 percent; availability of the knowledge management system must be 99.5 percent as a monthly average.

In short, using an outsourcing provider for design, development and delivery of learning has given the Accenture team more predictable costs and better service levels, while also providing ongoing access to deep skills and high-value consulting. The Accenture team kept the key planning functions in house, while also benefiting from the consultation of Accenture Learning. Vanthournout's team continues to determine the learning strategy and objectives, define the curricula and shape specific courses and solutions. But then the team can turn to its outsourcing partner to design, build and deliver the learning programs in the most cost-effective manner, always keeping in mind the phenomenal learning requirements already established.

The business payoff from advanced learning technologies

A final, extremely important component of the operational diagnosis for learning at Accenture had to do with the company's existing performance measurement and reporting tools to track learning design and delivery in a way that would ensure maximum cost effectiveness and maximum impact on the business. As Vanthournout recalls, "We needed to jumpstart our centralized reporting processes to manage our education investment more effectively. The existing infrastructure did not give us enough information on the use of newer modes of learning, such as Web-based training. Moreover, the growth of local training and learning programs meant that we could not keep an adequate handle on spending. We calculated that more than 30 percent of all delivery costs were not being captured in our reporting systems. Our learning investment decisions were being made too often in a vacuum." To address this issue, and to ensure that technology was leveraged both for cost and for the delivery of phenomenal learning, the team set out to identify, design and deliver the right mix of advanced learning technologies and decision support systems. That story is the basis of the next chapter.

The right kind of learning outsourcing relationship

Outsourcing any function usually begins as a cost play. But organizations that are advancing toward high performance today are looking at outsourcing—especially learning outsourcing—as something that delivers more than cost efficiencies. Outsourcing the learning function can deliver rapid business results that support growth: improvements in customer retention and satisfaction, increased speed to market of new products, improved productivity of strategic workforces such as IT, sales and customer call center operators, and decreased turnover of high-potential managers. Just as important, it can help an organization prepare for future challenges, helping it to continuously adapt and to drive innovation and growth.

The opportunity to get out ahead of the outsourcing trend comes in leveraging learning BPO as something richer and more complex than simply an attempt to save money in the back office of the learning operation. Cost savings are attractive in the short term; however, it is the transformational business impact of learning outsourcing that will sustain the relationship over time.

Graphing the different kinds of activities that fall loosely under the concept of learning BPO against the potential for transformational business impact, especially an impact on growth, one can see that many companies are only at the beginning of their journey to use learning outsourcing relationships to transform their businesses. As companies transfer increasingly more complex functions of their learning operations—from the learning management system to content design and delivery to strategic workforce development to enterprisewide learning—the opportunity increases for achieving transformational value and high performance.

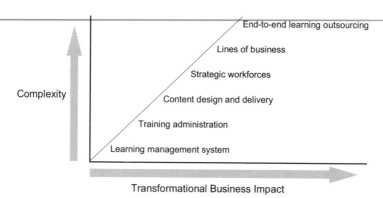

In other words, companies can get part way down the road to high performance with a focus on driving efficiency in the "non-core activities" of learning: the learning management system, learning administration, and so on. Make no mistake, these efficiencies are important and substantial. But really breaking through and using learning outsourcing to transform the business requires a more comprehensive relationship to address the core engine of learning and to drive innovation through the organization and its value chain.

Summary Points

- The "cost center" mentality about learning is a thing of the past. Learning organizations now must deliver business value and prove the business impact of learning investments.

- Senior management increasingly measures the performance of learning executives in terms of how well they manage the business side of learning, and how well they meet defined business outcomes.

- To address the increasing emphasis on business outcomes, today's learning professionals must have strong business skills. This is especially true for those people playing the Business Interlock role. Given the daily business decisions made for the curricula (for example, delivery vehicle, affordability, phenomenal criteria, etc.), strong business skills are a must.

- Running learning like a business requires mastery in at least three areas: plotting and measuring a journey toward upside value creation; governance and sponsorship; and efficiency planning and management.

- To improve operationally, a learning function needs to maximize the impact of different types of learning delivery mechanisms (e-learning versus CBT versus classroom) and make curriculum decisions based on the most appropriate delivery mechanism as well. Learning executives also must carefully define the learning department's core competencies, and define which aspects of work could be sourced externally to maximize both business impact and cost efficiency.

- Without effective operational strategies and mechanisms to deliver learning predictably and cost-effectively, even the best strategies and programs are not enough to ensure success.

- Operational improvements in learning can result by moving from a system of mass production to a system of custom, just-in-time production that responds to the changing needs of employees and the marketplace.

- The lifespan of learning content is shrinking as the marketplace changes more rapidly, so organizations must develop the means for faster and more efficient content production.
- Creating a supplier-client relationship by outsourcing learning design and delivery can result in high-quality learning with more predictable costs and better service levels.

Seven

Using Technology to Create a High-performance Learning Organization

The Accenture team had developed the necessary operational rigor to deliver phenomenal learning by the most cost-effective means possible. They had thought through the learning delivery and strategic sourcing issues that would help them run learning like a business. Now, the team turned to questions of implementation. And that put them squarely in Accenture's sweet spot: applying advanced and innovative information technologies for business advantage. The team looked to use technology in the most effective way possible to provide phenomenal learning, track learning delivery and results, and provide the information needed to support effective decision making about the learning function in the long term.

The shoemaker's children

New technologies are key to delivering learning in ways that are not only cost-effective but that also result in measurable improvements in workforce and business performance. At Accenture—a global management consulting, technology services and outsourcing company—certainly there was no shortage of innovative thinkers when it came to applying technology to learning. Nor was there a shortage of practical developers with deep expertise and experience. When it came to using technology to support its external clients, Accenture had few equals. The question was—bringing to mind the old story of the master shoemaker whose children had old, worn-out shoes—how was the state of Accenture's internal learning technology infrastructure?

In fact, the answer was mixed. Accenture had in place an internal system called the Training Management System (TMS), which had been years ahead of its time when it was first developed. It could handle functions such as course management and registration long before any learning management system vendors had even come into being. One option for Vanthournout and his team at Accenture might have been simply to leverage this existing system.

By 2000, however, Accenture's learning infrastructure had become fragmented and the TMS required a great deal of manual support. There was no concept of curricula or prescribed learning. Worst of all, the data was distributed over hundreds of databases worldwide. When employees transferred from one office to another, for example, their training files would need to be extracted, sent to the new database and then uploaded. Recalls Accenture's Samir Desai, "You can imagine the data integrity issues that caused for us. It was extremely difficult to perform any kind of centralized reporting on compliance or value. And managing any of the information centrally was time consuming and needed lots of manual support, so it was very expensive."

So the infrastructure already was somewhat shaky. What would happen when it became stressed by new demands and functions? Accenture's learning strategy now called for more e-learning to support the development of Accenture professionals. One risk was that the existing learning infrastructure would not hold up well under the strain Vanthournout's team was about to put on it.

Says John Ceisel, the business architect who guided the initial releases of the new learning infrastructure at Accenture, "It was clear from the start that if we had to support more than one infrastructure, we would not be successful from either a business standpoint or from the perspective of delivering phenomenal learning. The multiple infrastructures and overhead associated with that approach would have greatly increased our development and operations costs. More important, with multiple learning infrastructures, we would inevitably fall back into the fragmented approach to learning we'd had in the past."

Creating a single learning infrastructure would be a significant technical challenge, however. It meant creating one learning management system, one virtual instructor-led system and one learning data warehouse for all of Accenture, across dozens of countries and hundreds of business units. To meet this challenge, Vanthournout created what became known internally as the "Infrastructure Planning and Coordination team," composed of business architects who played a role similar to the Business Interlock role described in Chapter 5. This team, when assembled, had two key strengths: first, a balance of both business savvy and technical know-how; second, the desire to use technology not for technology's sake, but toward the goal of developing a learning infrastructure that really made a difference to how Accenture's people learned and worked. "We found early on," says Desai, "that while some developers only see technology as the bits and bytes, we saw it as the way to achieve our strategy and make a connection with our people. We wanted the 'phenomenality' of the learning experience to extend to the technology through which our people experienced learning and development."

Effective governance was as important here as it was to the overall learning transformation program. Notes Ceisel, "A critical factor in the team's success was identifying an advocate for each of our key stakeholders: business sponsors and management, as well as our employees. My role, representing the sponsors and their business requirements, is fairly obvious. Less typical, in my experience, was Don's decision to also have someone responsible for the personalization of the learning infrastructure, another individual responsible for reporting and, probably most intriguing, another team member responsible for the experience of the learners themselves. Toss in a lot of time and attention from Don as our team lead, and you had a highly effective team structured to ensure that the technology served the needs of all the stakeholders, including the often forgotten employee learners themselves."

A big challenge for Vanthournout's team was figuring out, based on all these inputs, which infrastructure business requirements were the most important. It would have been easy to fall into the trap of either relying on what existed in the current system or to make changes only according to who shouted the loudest. The key to avoiding either of these extremes was being guided at all times by the vision and strategy for learning that the team already had defined. The overall vision was the scale the technology team used to weigh requirements and to choose the most important ones. In a very short time, Ceisel and the team of business architects delivered on business requirements that met sponsors' needs, while ensuring alignment with the overall vision and strategy.

In addition, to achieve efficiencies and to help meet challenging delivery time frames, the team outsourced the development of the learning infrastructure to Accenture Learning. While the internal Accenture planning group could focus on business requirements and strategy, Accenture Learning had the resources and skills to focus on and overcome the many technical challenges to delivering a system that met these requirements. Recalls Ceisel, "We had the luxury of proceeding based on a fully funded business case, though naturally the funding was far less than we needed to fulfill the requests we received. We still needed to work with sponsors to understand the business impact of each request, prioritize requests based on their business impact and build consensus for the final requirements in each release. By partnering with a great team from Accenture Learning, we were able to focus on scoping the functional requirements to the associated business impact, without the distraction of the underlying technology implementation."

Nevertheless, even in outsourcing the deep technical skills, the Accenture team thought carefully about the higher-value functions they wanted to keep in house. "Although some of the functions could be outsourced," says Desai, "it was important for us to retain a core of information specialists who have the technical skills to effectively maintain our key systems, and who also have the business and relationship skills to work with customers to solve our constantly evolving business challenges."

What this all meant for the Accenture team was that, while many companies were (and are) struggling to implement one companywide learning management system, Accenture was able to perform that difficult task the first time out. The result was myLearning, Accenture's single and unified global learning management system. Because of myLearning, today any of Accenture's employees—more than 126,000 people in 48 countries—can go to a single intranet site for their learning and development needs. The new system created a single shared infrastructure for all virtual learning, one survey system to measure learning effectiveness, and one central data warehouse and decision support system for tracking and reporting.

"Deploying a global learning management system was a critical factor in the entire success story of reinventing learning at Accenture," reflects John Ceisel. "Retiring all the local training management systems allowed us to redeploy the associated local administrative personnel, representing more than $23 million in cost avoidance in the first three years and contributing to strong executive support for the business case." The fully funded business case allowed the team to build a global learning management system which, in almost all cases, exceeded the functionality of the local system, and also incorporated local training histories and local courses, which helped to generate strong local support. "Of course," quips Ceisel, "it didn't hurt that, in fact, we took a 'big bang' approach to implementation that shut down all of the local systems overnight. Certainly that also did a lot to ensure the new global system would be used!"

A comprehensive learning infrastructure at Accenture

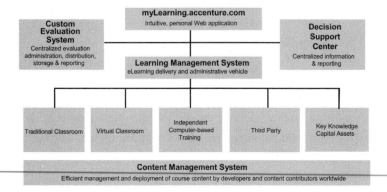

To respond to its global learning needs, Accenture created a unified, companywide infrastructure called myLearning that could coordinate the work of the decentralized business units to provide:

- Intuitive access to comprehensive information resources that enable Accenture professionals to be effective consumers of education based on both the company's and the individual's needs.
- Common, standardized delivery platforms for distributed education in order to reach Accenture employees closer to the job site, to minimize delivery costs and to allow the operating groups and business units to focus on education content instead of technical delivery.
- Common, consistent feedback from all learning assets, used to manage the quality of the content delivered to Accenture employees.
- Comprehensive reporting to improve management decision making and better align the overall education investment with business need.

Reaping the benefits

The myLearning system and a streamlined central operations team gave Accenture a means to address the centralization/decentralization issue that often plagues companies when it comes to learning management. The technology infrastructure for learning gave Accenture the best of both worlds: centralized control and local flexibility. Says Desai, "We would now be able to deal with situations where, for example, there would be a central requirement for an employee in Brazil to take a leadership course, though that person may have to go through a business approval process locally based on things like time, hours, content of the training and so forth. There could be a unified curriculum from one perspective, but also, at the same time, the ability for a local entity to put in controls and goals to meet local business needs." In Desai's words, "You can think of the overall technology infrastructure as the 'pipes' that deliver learning; but there also need to be the 'valves' that give you control over how much of what goes where. The myLearning system is the set of valves that gives us greater control today over what training gets pushed out in what amounts. That control capability has a huge impact on operational efficiency and value produced."

Another key aspect of the new operations and learning infrastructure for Accenture is the ability to support crucial training programs with wide global reach but also a high degree of central control. As Ceisel was driving out the core program, he came back with multifaceted requirements. The program needed to differ by workforce and by career level. It would be made up of multiple assets using multiple delivery channels. It would have complex rules around target audiences and exceptions. It would change often to meet changing business needs. All that the Accenture team needed to do was figure out how to deliver, track and measure such a program.

This core learning curriculum (see Chapter 2) is a key part of the Accenture learning strategy. In the past, however, delivering such a complex global program required a large central team and was very expensive. Today, by contrast, delivering global programs is a common part of everyday business for the central operations team. "Before myLearning," says Ceisel, "we needed a large group of HR professionals in each location to identify candidates for training who worked with those professionals to schedule them into the courses. Now, myLearning automates this entire process, from identifying the candidates based on the business rules, inviting them to register for a session or enrolling them directly if appropriate, and providing daily reports. Although business change is constant, the learning infrastructure lets us respond quickly as Accenture's business requirements continue to evolve."

For example, Sarbanes-Oxley and other regulations have placed a great deal of strain on many companies today. Statutory training has become mandatory, with high consequences for failure to comply. No company, including Accenture, can afford to be even 99 percent compliant; 100 percent is the only acceptable goal. So myLearning has allowed Accenture to deliver this type of mandatory training to all reaches of the globe, and then to track compliance to a 100 percent degree of accuracy. In the case of Sarbanes-Oxley training, for example, meeting the goal of 100 percent compliance required 378,715 course completions. In order to accomplish this, myLearning was leveraged to communicate to everyone that they needed to complete the training. And, because myLearning provided direct, on-demand access to the training, the course could be completed when it was most convenient to the employees. Because of myLearning, more than 60,000 course completions were recorded in three days, with accurate compliance reporting immediately available. For many companies, when it comes to compliance training, similar performance could take as long as a year.

Another key advantage of the new operations approach and learning infrastructure was its ability to support not just large learning programs offered at given points in time, but also continuous learning. Virtual classes have allowed Accenture to provide an effective and highly interactive way to support continuous learning through two types of educational programs to participants in different locations:

- Seminars, which address very timely and market-relevant content areas and which typically build content awareness among larger audiences. These virtual seminars frequently use a "radio show" format that actively engages learners.
- Workshops, which build deeper skills among smaller audiences. These workshops are typically longer in duration and allow students more opportunities to collaborate with each other and to interact with instructors.

Although not a substitute for the cultural assimilation benefits of the common learning curriculum at the central training facility used by Accenture, these virtual seminars and workshops proved wildly successful. Learning communities organized series of seminars around hot topics, leveraging the knowledge of experienced Accenture executives. Professionals could attend such a seminar without traveling from their work locations, or they could listen to recorded versions of the seminars if their schedules did not permit attendance at the original live event. Thus, in various ways, the myLearning system has removed one of the biggest barriers to effective corporate learning: access. As long as Accenture employees have access to a computer, they also have access to thousands of Accenture's learning assets and experiences.

The myLearning system has had other related effects—on costs, for example. While many of the learning assets at Accenture are built internally, some are brought in from third-party vendors and integrated into the overall program. With the myriad of different technical standards and platforms, integration of third-party content might have been very costly. With myLearning, however, Accenture was able to define a common vendor interface that allows Accenture people seamless access to thousands of vendor courses. The myLearning capabilities enable Accenture to effectively track actual course usage to optimize vendor contracts—that is, to determine costs on actual course completion, not just on course availability. It also allows Accenture to manage the effectiveness of the vendor assets to ensure that the quality is at the level expected for its people.

By presenting a common and consistent face for learning at Accenture, myLearning has also enabled the company to have a single, common channel for global communications to the workforce. "The communications benefit of our single learning channel is substantial," says Desai. "It is one thing to have a strategy and to have developed the learning assets. It's quite another thing to get thousands of people worldwide to understand it and what it all means for them personally. The myLearning system has allowed us to communicate in one voice effectively and inexpensively."

Managing assets as a portfolio

One of the ongoing questions any learning team faces is how to manage all the assets it is creating. At Accenture, as learning assets continued to proliferate, it was important to employ a process for managing the life cycle of the assets. The answer was to create and then monitor a feedback loop. Using myLearning's evaluation system, all learning assets delivered at Accenture, including vendor courses, are now followed up with a standard survey—one survey with the same questions. Previously, each learning asset had different surveys by which feedback was obtained— questions typically defined by the course owner's priorities. In many cases these surveys were not even automated. That meant it was almost impossible to analyze the evaluations or even compare them meaningfully. Decision makers could not know whether one learning asset was working better than another. Now, with a common scale of evaluation, the various sponsors for a learning asset can analyze their entire portfolio of assets on an equal basis.

The course evaluation data captured provides a wealth of information that forms the basis for making fact-based decisions about the curricula. As Olson notes, "The myLearning evaluation system provides us with a wealth of data that was simply unimaginable previously. Our solution planners, performing Business Interlock activities, can now do more than just help make the upfront decisions about curricula and courses. They can use the evaluation data to make solid, ongoing business decisions that continuously shape and improve our curricula. This data allows us to fulfill our commitment to phenomenal training, as well as keep our content relevant to our target audiences."

In addition, for many of Accenture's strategic learning assets, the myLearning reporting functions allow decision makers to drill down to a lower and more granular level of data to help determine cause and effect more clearly. If there is a problem with one class module that meets from 3:00 to 5:00 p.m. on day 3 of a two-week course, managers can see the problem and correct it on a timely basis. "We have learned," says Ceisel, that phenomenal learning isn't something that occurs only once in time. It's an ongoing process. The feedback loops we created allow us to improve our assets continuously."

Decision support

Other kinds of management support also have been enabled by the myLearning system. The "myLearning Decision Support" function integrates information from a variety of sources and provides a customized, comprehensive and timely snapshot of learning metrics. This reporting function is essential for the learning professionals as well as for executives outside of the learning space.

For Desai, leveraging technology solutions in a way that could help align learning with the business had been a key interest for several years. He had begun his career with Accenture in learning development. In that role, as he says, "I kept coming back to questions about what impact we were really having from our learning programs. We were developing courses for people based on what we believed to be gaps in their knowledge and performance. But were we right? Had we made a difference to the individuals and to the company as a whole? It was always hard to know, because we had no way of globally tracking or understanding what was going on from the perspective of business impact."

Although almost every organization sees the value in having actionable learning information, they often do not give decision support the same attention and energy they give to using technology for the transactional part of the learning infrastructure. That mindset often results from thinking only about cost savings, and not about the additional value that can be created through technology-supported learning. Vanthournout saw the value-creating possibilities very early on and was willing to request the resources needed to develop the decision support capability.

To incorporate robust decision support capabilities into myLearning, the Accenture team first identified the key learning stakeholders in the company, and then determined what information these individuals needed in order to make better education investment decisions. They then extended the company's enterprise learning solution to capture the most relevant data from various repositories and tailored this information to meet the needs of critical user groups. As with other parts of the total learning solution, the Accenture team leveraged its outsourcing relationship with Accenture Learning to its advantage. By outsourcing aspects of the development of the decision support tool, Desai was able to focus on the business questions and metrics while the architects and developers at Accenture Learning were able to focus on building out a robust learning data warehouse.

The resulting decision support system was a huge benefit to Accenture, says Desai. "We were now able to have centralized and timely information to support faster decision making based on facts. The system could give us metrics that were aligned with business goals. We could not have done that without having a central system where we collected that information. That was part of my role: to figure out how to collect that information, how to report on it, what metrics to report, and then to roll it out through all different levels of the organization."

Today, Accenture's learning stakeholders—from company executives to learning sponsors—can make more informed education investment decisions using the myLearning decision support tool. Customized reporting features allow user groups to examine their learning programs from a variety of perspectives and, most important, make appropriate modifications. As Andy White says, "We now have more information about who is going to learning programs, what we spend and what the learning results are. Because of that, we can be smarter about where we spend our training dollars and how much we spend."

Desai himself frequently sees the benefits of Accenture's decision support capability. "We've been in meetings where there has been either a disagreement about the facts, or a situation where no one has known the exact facts—and that was preventing us from moving forward on something. In the past, we might have commissioned a 'study' to look into the issue—which is not only costly and time-consuming, but also prone to get ignored because results often get delivered too late to answer the original question. Today, right there during the meeting, we can access from our laptop PCs the decision support capability of myLearning, get the facts and then use them to help drive the group toward a decision. Sometimes it's almost like being able to align learning with the business in real time. You can make better decisions because you're dealing with facts at your fingertips."

Vanthournout adds, "In my role as chief learning officer, I am regularly challenged by our executives with questions or recommended changes based on anecdotal information they may have heard. With the myLearning Decision Support system, I can quickly turn those exchanges into fact-based discussions in real time, so that we are making business decisions grounded in reality and not emotion. And, with the automation we have put in place, not only can I get the information much faster, but I can do so at a much lower cost than having teams of people perform ad hoc analyses."

White, too, notes that, "There's nothing like a few facts to shed light on things sometimes." He recalls one occasion when senior executives from one of Accenture's geographic areas wanted to build their own training center in their region because they felt that employees from their areas weren't learning enough or getting enough value during their visits to the St. Charles campus. "Well," said White, "all we had to do was go to the myLearning site and look at how students from that region had performed, how they had rated the courses and how they had assessed their learning experience. In fact, the numbers indicated that, by and large, participants felt their experiences at the central learning events were hugely important to them, and that they had learned as much as students from other regions. The hard data we accessed through myLearning's evaluation system allowed us to provide the counsel back to the practice which, in my opinion at least, saved our company and our shareholders from an expense that wasn't really necessary."

Three keys to a successful learning decision support system

According to Samir Desai, who helped lead and manage the myLearning decision support system for Accenture, companies should focus on creating learning decision support systems that provide information that is:

- **Accurate.** For public companies, regulatory issues mean that data related to compliance issues must be 100 percent accurate. But even for data not specifically related to compliance, Accenture strove for accuracy exceeding 98 percent.
- **Accessible.** Data can be accurate, but if you can't get at it when you need it, it might as well not exist at all. Accenture Learning has driven availability of information exceeding 98.5 percent. In addition, the decision support system includes one global website that gives global and local entities access to the same information.
- **Actionable.** Finally, the data needs to be aligned with metrics that are aligned with business questions that are aligned with the business strategy. Data also needs

to be current enough to align with the decision-making cycle. Having data just for the sake of data is sometimes worse than having no data at all.

As Desai says, "When you meet these three criteria—accurate, accessible and actionable—you end up with a high level of trust among your executive decision makers. They are confident they can get the right information, when and where they need it. When that happens, the conversations don't focus on whether people agree about the data, but instead on what people can do *with* the data."

Taking it to the next level

The experiences of the Accenture team in delivering phenomenal learning and incorporating leading-edge technologies to enhance the learning experience, all while delivering substantial cost savings, emboldened them to take the next step: expand the influence of the learning organization into the knowledge management arena.

- One key to a successful global learning infrastructure is to balance business savvy and technical know-how, on the one hand, with the benefit of that technology in supporting actual performance needs. Technology does not exist for its own sake, but to support a learning infrastructure that makes a difference to people.
- The technical portion of a major learning change program must be guided at all times by the business vision and strategy.
- Even when outsourcing the technical aspects of learning, organizations will want to consider the information specialists to retain in-house, to meet ongoing technology and business challenges.
- An effective technology infrastructure for learning gives organizations both centralized control and local flexibility.
- A global electronic learning capability can dramatically improve the ability of companies to meet many of today's needs in areas like compliance training.
- A global learning infrastructure can integrate vital decision-support functionalities that help increase the impact of learning and keep it aligned with the most important business needs.
- An effective decision support system is one where information delivered is accurate, accessible and actionable.

▸ *Eight*

At the Frontiers of Learning and Knowledge Sharing

It's the morning of June 13, 2005. Don Vanthournout and Jill Smart, along with their entire capability development team, are watching with anticipation as the global Accenture organization flips a virtual switch, shutting down one knowledge management platform and cutting over to another. The new "Accenture Knowledge Exchange" would immediately give Accenture employees around the world instant access to an improved system for organizing, accessing and sharing knowledge and experience.

The new knowledge management and sharing system at Accenture was a technological accomplishment that only a few people might ever fully appreciate. In an expedited time frame, all while keeping the existing knowledge management system fully functional, a team led by Tom Barfield, an experienced senior manager on Vanthournout's team, had successfully ported the entire global Accenture organization from its existing Lotus Notes platform for knowledge management to a new Microsoft platform. This migration had required integrating or replacing more than 100 different knowledge management applications and content storage repositories that had sprung up over time around the company's global practice.

In the background of this huge accomplishment is an important question that needs to be asked: why was Vanthournout's group at Accenture (the team in charge of learning and training) running a knowledge management project—the global rollout of a complex effort to develop a new taxonomy of knowledge at Accenture, and then to design the technology solution to revolutionize knowledge sharing throughout the company? Offering an adequate answer to that question, it turns out, is important for understanding how organizations today can truly deliver a "return on learning."

Who's managing knowledge?

At the dawn of the 21st century, the idea of what "learning" really means is changing dramatically. Today's students go to school and sit in classrooms for the greater part of the day. It's not always tremendously efficient, but they're learning, right? No one wants to question that. They listen to lectures, work in small groups, answer questions, take tests. Then they go home for the day. They conduct online searches to research material with which to write a paper or complete a homework assignment. They get on their instant messaging programs and converse with friends about an assignment they're working on (and, yes, share a bit of gossip along the way). Someone may have missed class that day, or not been paying attention, so one person might e-mail class notes so a friend can complete the day's assignment and not fall too far behind.

Are these students learning?

Well, sure. Why would one say otherwise? It would not only be supremely arrogant for teachers to claim that learning only occurs when they are around, it would be counter to everything known about cognitive science—about how the human brain takes in, synthesizes and retains information. Why is it that the human memory may hold little, if any, recollection of a lecture heard years ago, but still maintain a distinct and sharp memory of an idle remark made in the school hallway by a friend just after class?

In a corporate environment, too, the traditional line between learning, on the one hand, and knowledge sharing, on the other, is becoming extremely difficult to draw. The blending of learning, knowledge sharing, collaboration and performance support is now beginning to be reflected not only in applications and technologies, but in organizational structures, too. A degree of top-down learning activities—courses planned by a central group to meet a set of common workforce performance and business needs—is as vital as ever to corporate success. Increasingly, however, organizations are asking employees to take a greater share of responsibility for gaining the knowledge and skills they need to do their jobs. Why? Because in a rapidly changing marketplace, employees with a certain degree of experience often know better than anyone what they know, what they don't know and what they need to know. Knowledge sharing is how a savvy organization makes possible the kinds of employee-driven learning experiences that separate high performers from the rest of the pack, and which increasingly will be necessary for success in the coming years.

Much of the learning reinvention story at Accenture to this point has been about driving top-down kinds of learning experiences—doing so in an innovative fashion, maximizing the impact of learning on the business, using a core curriculum to recapture Accenture's common culture, and driving more effective and efficient learning, and better decision making, through advanced technologies. The development of innovative and phenomenal learning experiences, the creation of the myLearning infrastructure—those are the prescribed learning events and tools that were identified and developed to create successful Accenture professionals who can contribute to the company's success.

But Jill Smart, Don Vanthournout and the rest of the Accenture team knew full well that much more was needed to keep Accenture on top in its marketplace. Learning executives cannot anticipate every business and performance need for workers today, and then create formal learning events targeted at those needs. So to create more effective employee-driven learning experiences, Accenture sought to upgrade its knowledge sharing technologies and capabilities. And, because Accenture properly saw knowledge sharing as *another kind of learning,* senior management made the decision to fold the knowledge sharing initiative under Vanthournout's responsibilities.

This new organizational structure at Accenture, where learning and knowledge management are driven by the same management team, represents an identifiable trend today. In an Accenture Learning research initiative into high-performance learning organizations, large percentages of the learning executives surveyed noted that they are integrating (or have immediate plans to integrate) their learning initiatives with related endeavors such as knowledge sharing and performance support.

This organizational structure reflects changing attitudes toward technology and knowledge management. It is no longer automatically the case that knowledge sharing is overseen by a technology manager; increasingly there is oversight by functional leads like HR and training or learning. Accenture is a case in point. A traditional leader and pioneer in the field of knowledge management, Accenture has for eight consecutive years been designated a global "Most Admired Knowledge Enterprise" and is now in the top three most-admired companies globally. But consider the significance organizationally of who originally owned responsibility for the Knowledge Exchange, the primary knowledge management system at Accenture. In the early 1990s, that responsibility fell to the chief information officer. One can see why: when the knowledge management challenge was considered to be primarily technological—designing and implementing the actual technology network—the head of technology should direct the implementation and maintenance of the network. By 2000, though, knowledge management had come to be understood not just in terms of technology but in terms of the business capabilities it supported. Beyond the technical infrastructure were the real business reasons for knowledge sharing: decision making, innovation and superior service to clients. The knowledge management system was a "just-in-time" learning tool, above all. And, accordingly, the responsibility for knowledge management moved to the human resources function.

Learning solutions that look like knowledge sharing ... and vice versa

Evolving organizational structures, however, would not make sense were it not for the fact that, increasingly, technology-based solutions in learning are beginning to look like knowledge sharing solutions and vice versa. One leading consumer electronics retailer, for example, has been working with Accenture Technology Labs on a solution that uses content management systems and leading-edge technologies to deliver product information to sales people in real time, right on the sales floor. As these applications mature, customers will get better service and the sales people will need less external classroom training. The company can put new hires on the sales floor and have them perform at acceptable levels more quickly than ever before. Are these solutions learning solutions? Knowledge management? Performance support? They are all of them, at once.

Or consider the kinds of blended learning and knowledge management applications that are now increasingly showing up at call centers and other functions with customer-facing roles. There, those who sell to and service customers require the most up-to-date information available, and they don't necessarily have time to take a training course each time there is a new product available. Knowledge portals are helping to bring vital product, service and procedural information together into a single structured content architecture that gives call center agents easier access to vital information to serve customers more effectively.

And behind the organizational and technology changes that are enabling a blend of learning and knowledge management sits the most important driver: underlying business changes—especially a marketplace and economic environment that are changing so rapidly that organizations do not always have time for formal or traditional training design. When they enter new markets, for example, organizations need to act quickly to support the performance of their people. Early in the life cycle of a domain or content area, companies cannot afford the time (and cost) to invest in building structured training opportunities. For those situations, they need to make sure people in the business units can more readily share knowledge so they can, in effect, learn from each other. Organizations also need to be able to capture emerging experiences, store them digitally and make them accessible to everyone. However, as a domain or content area matures and grows, there comes a time when organizations can harvest the experiences of people in the business units into more structured training if the marketplace needs still warrant.

A vision for learning and knowledge management at Accenture

The possibilities of more effective integration of learning and knowledge management—and the potential impact on workforce performance and on Accenture's business and competitive environment—were critical to Vanthournout's thinking, and to the work of his learning transformation team, as he added knowledge management to his responsibilities in 2002. One of Vanthournout's first decisions in the knowledge management arena was to fold it under the identical steering committee and governance structure already in place to oversee and direct the learning transformation at Accenture (for more, see Chapter 4). Integrating knowledge management and learning, and directing them toward the same workforce and business needs, had a better chance of success if both could be led by the same team and governed by the same executive committee. Then Vanthournout charged Tom Barfield, the new global knowledge management lead for Accenture, with developing an initial series of recommendations about the future of knowledge management to present to that steering committee.

For Barfield, effective knowledge management comes down to a few key goals. "We at Accenture—and, I would argue, every enterprise today—want to tap into the collective knowledge and experience of our people for three reasons in particular: to enhance revenue, create better efficiencies to drive out wasted time and excessive costs, and to foster innovation."

Achieving those goals meant, first, that the Accenture team had to look at the changing revenue patterns for the company overall, and at the workforce structure that would best support its business strategy. In the long term, the Accenture business was moving toward a different mix of its traditional consulting, technology and outsourcing businesses. Accenture saw continued momentum in growing the outsourcing portfolio of business faster than the consulting work. This change would have discernible effects on who was doing client work, where it was done and what tools and supporting structures would be necessary for Accenture employees to learn, collaborate and perform optimally. As discussed in Chapter 2, the Accenture workforce was becoming far less monolithic, reflecting different client needs. Though the Consulting workforce was continuing to grow, the Solutions workforce, focused on deploying reusable technology solutions, and the Services workforce, managing specialized operations for long-term outsourcing engagements, were growing much more rapidly. Many in the Solutions and Services workforce are centralized into delivery center locations worldwide, creating a more efficient way of directing the best employees to the right client needs, wherever they are located.

So as Barfield and team looked to Accenture's needs, both in terms of its business model and the workforce and delivery structure necessary to execute that model, the importance of supporting employee performance and development in new ways was clear. "In the past," notes Barfield, "our people focused on building deep expertise in a given area that was fairly static. Now, we were promising our leadership that we would support both general and specialized skills in our different workforces, including emerging skills and content areas, to drive business results. That led us to an integrated approach to knowledge management and learning. You can't separate the two if your focus is on the business need or potential business impact. You need both."

Another way to approach the need for better knowledge management and knowledge sharing is to consider how a company like Accenture can have the maximum impact on the growth and performance of it employees, who are almost all knowledge workers. In any given year, Accenture employees receive approximately 80 to 120 hours of training. That sounds like a lot, although in fact it translates to around five percent of their time. Vanthournout's team knew it could achieve greater impact on the performance of workers—that is, their ability to serve clients in an exceptional way, regardless of which of the workforces they operated in—by reaching employees during the other 95 percent of their time as well. As Barfield says, "It is not effective for people to have to stop and disengage from work each time they need guidance, information or support. Knowledge and learning have to be accessed and delivered in the natural course of an employee's work."

Accordingly, as the Accenture team thought about its people enablement strategy (see Figure 1), it added a layer of performance support, knowledge management support and collaboration with peers to the existing structure of courses, scheduling, performance management and feedback. In the end, the effect was to drive the organization to get closer to employees at the point where they need support performing their jobs.

A knowledge management and delivery mindset can also use lower-cost delivery channels to provide knowledge to people when it is needed. When the only solutions available are training solutions, everything can tend to look like a training problem. By integrating knowledge management and learning, it is possible to achieve the same (or sometimes better) results through lower-cost knowledge management delivery channels. And, given that Vanthournout and team now had responsibility for all of these channels, there were no longer any debates about whether something was a learning initiative or a knowledge management initiative.

Cognitive scientists have been saying for years that performance needs and context drive learning retention. A "just-in-case" approach to learning can lead to situations where employees retain very little of the information they receive in a training course. It's as if you're storing water in a leaky bucket; by the time you need the water, the bucket is empty. But a "just-in-time" approach to

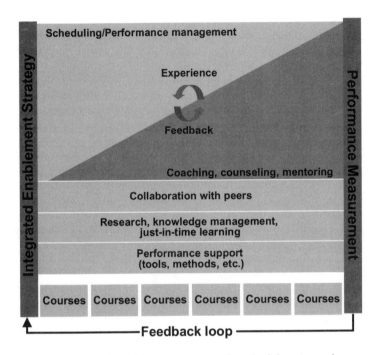

Figure 1. Accenture's enablement strategy reflects both learning and knowledge management emphases

learning—which is at the heart of a knowledge management and knowledge sharing strategy today—not only leads to more effective performance at that moment, but also to greater retention of the knowledge and experience, so future performance of the same task will also be better.

Operational challenges

Even with a more effective enablement strategy in place, Barfield was aware of the challenges he faced—both organizationally and technologically—in devising and implementing a new vision for knowledge management at Accenture. The same challenging economic conditions that had led to a temporary decline in the effectiveness of learning at Accenture had affected the knowledge management organization as well. In recent years, a more central-ized approach to knowledge management had been implemented as a way of becoming more cost efficient. Developers of the many knowledge management applications around the company had been centralized in one team, and a global sourcing and shared services model had been implemented, using capabilities in Manila and India.

Increased efficiency had not, unfortunately, created more effec-tive knowledge management and sharing. The various organiza-tional units had remained extremely siloed in their approaches to knowledge sharing. In more prosperous times, Accenture had the luxury of assigning "knowledge managers" to oversee the harvest-ing of experiences from client work, writing up those experiences and posting them to the Knowledge Exchange. As the economy worsened, some 30 percent of these managers had left the company or been laid off. Without these "valves" in place to manage the flow of knowledge, content of uncertain quality and value had proliferated. One internal estimate was that more than 200,000 items of questionable value resided in the knowledge management system. Managing the archival content—something that had not previously been done consistently across organizational groups—now was not being done at all.

"We have high expectations for ourselves at Accenture," says Barfield. "Based on external benchmarks, we were still a global leader in knowledge management. But try telling that to our em-ployees out in the field, who were growing increasingly frustrated as they tried to find the information they needed." In Accenture's annual employee satisfaction survey, questions about knowledge management began eliciting some negative responses. "We knew," Barfield says, "we had a long way to go."

Building trust and expertise

Barfield and Vanthournout strategized about the best way to pro-ceed. A big part of their initial challenge, they felt, was in establishing trust with all the various knowledge management teams around the world. "To a number of people around the practice," Barfield recalls, "those of us in the global, centralized team were outsiders. There wasn't a high degree of trust anywhere—trust in the global team or trust between the various knowledge management teams. So we decided that we had to do something so that the many knowledge management teams would feel more comfortable looking to us for leadership, and so that we could all work better together, as well. We needed a quick win to demonstrate our capabilities."

What Barfield and his team did was to leverage the existing capabilities of the myLearning infrastructure to create an enterprise search capability, common across Accenture's content delivery tools. The integrated search function allows a user to type a keyword into any of the applications and then receive relevant resources from all support channels: these include learning and knowledge management, discussion databases and access to more than 13,000 people considered to have distinctive experience in various content areas. In addition to providing the technical integration between the learning and knowledge management applications, this approach also helped to break down the walls between the learning and knowledge management organizations.

At the same time, Barfield and Vanthournout sought to understand what was and was not working well with the knowledge management system that had evolved at Accenture through the 1990s. The Accenture team surveyed more than 300 end users to understand their perspectives. The biggest problem, it turns out, was that users of the system were confused: there were so many knowledge sharing applications and so much content that the users didn't know where to start to find information they needed. The system was too complicated.

These survey results were shared during a meeting of about two dozen leaders and knowledge management pioneers at Accenture during a virtual strategy session. A strong consensus emerged from this meeting that, both in terms of process and technology, a new global knowledge management system was required. And that meant a major migration from the existing technology infrastructure.

The great migration

The existing infrastructure for knowledge management at Accenture was both a blessing and a curse. With a distinguished heritage in knowledge management, Accenture had a rich repository of knowledge and content. But it was located in an infrastructure that was becoming obsolete. Over time, the knowledge management approach of the legacy system—based on disparate databases—had led to a great deal of both redundant and conflicting content. Users might alter a document in one database, but those changes would fail to properly replicate across all other instances of the content. These databases were also being partly replaced and partly augmented by Web-based portals. In spite of attempts to maintain centralized access through a centralized Accenture portal, the fact that other decentralized portals lurked throughout the environment meant that it could be confusing to find the most relevant and up-to-date information about a subject. Organizationally, decentralization also meant that it had become difficult to determine who ultimately should be responsible for managing the various categories of content. These were the conditions that had elicited some of the blunt, negative feedback about the existing knowledge management system from Accenture employees around the world.

Barfield's group, working closely with the CIO organization, began developing and implementing a new Knowledge Exchange in 2004. The team first developed an overall architecture based on Microsoft SharePoint technology (see Figure 2), which would eliminate the existing, decentralized Lotus Notes environment, with its independent knowledge-sharing tools that had become factionalized throughout the global practice. In its place were new design principles: to leverage existing and packaged software and extend the basic SharePoint structure only when absolutely necessary to support a business-critical need.

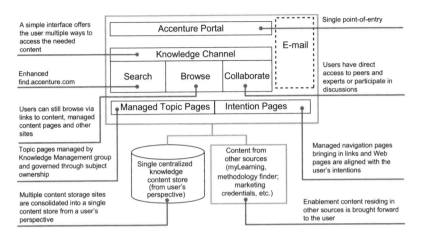

Figure 2. Accenture's high-level view of its new knowledge management architecture

The solution would focus on a set of core capabilities related to a document repository, expertise directory, topic area and search functionality. The solution was designed to be simple, cost-efficient and effective, but also incremental—delivered and improved over a series of phased releases. As Vanthournout put it, "Our attitude was, let's not try to build the 'perfect' knowledge management application right away. If we take that approach we'll never get started. Let's get a working solution out there and then iterate based on real experience so that changes we make will truly be based on how the system is being used."

Another key to success that came out of Accenture's earlier experience was to design the system from the perspective of the employees using it. Information systems have not always been friendly to the people using them; they often have been difficult to use, requiring basic training even just to navigate through the functions. To avoid that pitfall, the team developed an end-user strategy to ensure that the design of the user interface would allow users to navigate naturally and intuitively to content, resources and services.

The basic organizing structure for the content in the system—called the "taxonomy"—was vital to the success of the new system.

The team had developed an initial organizing principle for documents, focused on what business processes were being supported, so that it would be easier for employees to find relevant information. Vanthournout and Barfield were anxious to avoid a situation where document descriptions were tied to specific labels for groups. As Barfield notes, "If 'consultant-speak'—jargon and words that go out of style quickly—got into the structure, this would ultimately have a negative effect on finding knowledge and experience." Keeping the organizing principles more generic might also help limit duplication of content, as knowledge bases that would be contributed to by more than one organization unit could be consolidated rather than managed along departmental lines.

The team also wrestled with a familiar issue in knowledge management: what to do about obsolete knowledge found in aging documents stored in the repository. Here, one of the unintended consequences of migrating Accenture from one knowledge management platform to another turned out to be beneficial: not every knowledge item would be carried over. This was the perfect opportunity to "retire" documents that usage and access statistics showed were rarely or never used. Like people moving to a new house who use the change in address as an excuse to throw out their "junk," the transition to a new knowledge management platform allowed Accenture to mine the golden nuggets from the raw material currently in its knowledge repositories—and to discard the dross.

Successful governance principles for knowledge management

One of the things that Barfield and his team learned through their experience in rejuvenating knowledge management at Accenture is that the governance principles are in some respects almost diametrically opposed to the governance structures that led to so much success in the overall learning initiative. With learning, as noted in earlier chapters, a top-down governance structure was required to push through essential organizational change. With knowledge management, on the other hand, Barfield notes that, "We couldn't take a governance approach driven only from the top, with reduced involvement from the individual groups. Instead, what worked was a bottom-up governance approach. The individual organizational groups were involved with all decisions—building relationships and working together to a common solution."

The governance structure used was what is often referred to as a "federated" model: individual groups delegate authority to the central knowledge management group on a set of specific issues, while they also operate independently on others. So, for example, the central group maintained authority for things like overall knowledge management strategy, the technology infrastructure, metrics, standards and compliance. The local groups, on the other hand, remained in charge of things like sales and delivery support in their areas, content acquisition and development and finding and accrediting experts.

Says Barfield, "This federated approach has helped us realize a number of benefits in terms of aligning our organization, reducing costs, establishing management accountability and accelerating the business results. We have the flexibility to accommodate variations in workforce attributes, markets, attitudes and geographies, and that lets people get the kinds of knowledge they prefer and really need. At the same time we get better overall control where it's needed and appropriate. We reduce risk through centralized control, but we can also be more innovative by using the local entities as testing grounds for new programs."

In the end, though, it is the impact on the business that counts. As Vanthournout notes, "In almost every conversation with our clients, we make the pitch that an individual client team brings to bear the experience of all of Accenture's people around the world. With the new Knowledge Exchange, we can point to the way we actually make that happen."

What's on the horizon?

Next up for knowledge management at Accenture: continuing the drive toward high performance through integrated learning and knowledge management. Three initiatives are primary:

- Improve the ability for people to connect with and learn from each other.
- Integrate the myLearning and Knowledge Exchange infrastructures.
- Create knowledge sharing solutions for specific business critical roles.

Improving the ability for people to connect with and learn from each other

Knowledge sharing is not just about finding a document in a repository. Most of the knowledge at Accenture is not housed in a database, but rather in the minds of Accenture's people. But in order to tap into that knowledge—what academics call "tacit" knowledge—a company needs to foster effective social networks within the organization. Today at Accenture, creating and maintaining those networks is accomplished through creating expert profiles, communities of practice and discussion forums. In the coming months and years, Vanthournout's team intends to improve on those approaches by, for example, simplifying the process people must follow to build and maintain their expert profile. Although 13,000 people at Accenture currently have profiles, this is a small percentage of the overall Accenture workforce. And many people find it too difficult to update their profiles; if profiles are out of date, that can damage the trust people feel in the system itself. So, today, Barfield is pursuing ways to simplify the maintenance process, and then is looking to design the systems in such a way that experts are not overwhelmed with inquiries. Being an expert isn't just an honor: it involves work, too, so the key is to find the right balance—enough work so experts feel they are making a contribution, but not so much to prevent them from doing the primary job to which they have been assigned.

Communities of practice—which originally were put in place at Accenture in 1995—are groups of people who work together toward a common goal, whether that is learning from each other or developing new business opportunities. Over the past decade or so, about 150 of these communities have been created, and they have grown organically with little or no central support or coordination. That has resulted in inconsistencies in how these groups are led, which has in turn led to unevenness in their effectiveness and success. The knowledge management team at Accenture is now working on ways to give communities better guidance, particularly for knowing the best time to create a group; managing the group; and measuring the group's success. By improving these communities, Accenture will improve the ability of its people to learn from each other.

Integration of the myLearning and Knowledge Exchange infrastructures

One of the initial decisions that supported the integration of learning and knowledge management at Accenture was extending the search capability created in myLearning to include the company's knowledge sharing applications. And a key aspect of the reinvention of learning and knowledge management was the development of a topic-based taxonomy to organize the knowledge content. Barfield and his knowledge management team are bringing this endeavor full circle, back to myLearning, by implementing the knowledge management taxonomy within the myLearning system. "This," says Barfield, "will allow us to more easily tie together the content housed within the two systems. When people using the myLearning system find a particular course, they will be shown related knowledge assets and experts. And vice versa: a user of the Knowledge Exchange who is accessing a knowledge area will see a list of learning assets that relate to that search. This will blur the lines between learning and knowledge sharing even further. And that's a good thing."

Creation of knowledge sharing solutions for specific business-critical roles

The new Knowledge Exchange system has established a strong foundation for general knowledge sharing across Accenture, but it remains a "one-size-fits-all" approach. While the system will continue to evolve in terms of these common capabilities, the knowledge management team increasingly will focus on supporting those Accenture roles that stand to benefit the most from knowledge sharing—and whose performance, aided by more effective knowledge sharing, stands to have the most impact on the company's overall performance and the solutions it delivers to its clients. These tailored knowledge sharing solutions, or "performance workspaces," will be created to support people in those key roles. (See box.)

The next generation of knowledge portals: the performance workspace

Knowledge portals have been an important development in connecting people with the knowledge they need to do their jobs. However, many portals today are targeted to provide a thin layer of information to the broadest base of employees in the company. They do not proactively deliver tailored information to the right people at the right time to meet specific performance needs. As a result, many organizations are looking for a more effective and strategic workforce enabler: real-time, active support for the performance of their most important workers, integrated across all essential resources and supporting applications. Such support should also be tied to an enterprisewide performance management capability that links differentiated individual performance to higher workforce performance and, ultimately, to the performance of the organization as a whole.

These capabilities can now be delivered in what is called a "performance workspace." A performance workspace is a comprehensive solution that delivers a workforce-specific, role-based desktop environment made up of the knowledge, content, legacy applications, productivity tools, learning, collaboration and expert network capabilities that enable workers to increase their performance to new levels.

A performance workspace integrates eight performance accelerators, each tailored to a specific job or role:

1. **Performance management.** These solutions motivate better performance by tying personal success to group and corporate success. A performance workspace includes individual and organizational objectives, coupled with real-time monitoring of critical metrics proven to increase performance, such as targets, incentives and bonus calculators.
2. **Process support.** With integrated process flows, methodologies, procedures and task support, a performance workspace can dramatically improve process efficiencies, cut cycle time and reduce risk.
3. **Collaboration.** Collaborative applications and work areas support capabilities such as "expert-intensive" solution design, team-based development of work products, and program status reporting and issue tracking—all of which can foster innovation and better decision making.
4. **Discovery and access to experienced resources.** By finding and linking workers to experienced colleagues in a particular content area, "people connections" are improved, the ability to transfer roles or take on difficult assignments is increased and, most important, customer service can reflect the best knowledge and experience the organization has to offer.
5. **Performance development.** A performance workspace delivers high-impact, just-in-time learning experiences that can dramatically reduce training delivery costs, improve knowledge retention and speed time to competency.
6. **Knowledge base.** By managing and delivering customized knowledge about customers, products, services, applications and a host of other items, a performance workspace can enable the sharing of leading practices and bring all relevant knowledge together to support performance.
7. **Access to applications.** With single sign-on access to relevant applications, integrated into a single view, workers can improve their service levels to all stakeholders and increase their productivity.

8. **Search.** A robust search capability, using natural language query, helps workers save time and improve decision making by connecting key information across silos.

Together, these accelerators improve the ability of today's mission-critical workforces to contribute to growth, innovation and high performance.

◆————————————————◆

Beyond technology

The ongoing knowledge management initiatives at Accenture are indicative of a key trend: an increased focus on the non-technology aspects of knowledge management. Barfield has found that with the technology infrastructure in place, the knowledge management team can now be much more effective because it can focus on what should be accomplished through knowledge management and knowledge sharing from a business and workforce perspective. "We've only just begun to see the kinds of measurable benefits from knowledge management that we proved we had with learning," says Barfield. In fact, Tad Waddington, who directed the groundbreaking learning ROI study for Accenture, now has turned his attention to knowledge management. "The initial ROI findings, frankly, are nowhere near where they can be," says Barfield. "But that simply reflects the fact that the field of knowledge management is less mature. We know we have to leverage our experts throughout the company better; we have to manage the content we have better. We have to increase the number of knowledgeable employees contributing to our Knowledge Exchange."

Above all, Accenture continues to work on improving its culture of knowledge sharing. And that's a matter of encouraging the right kinds of behaviors. As Barfield puts it, "Certainly we had to have the new knowledge management technologies to help accelerate our ability to share knowledge and collaborate successfully. But ultimately our success will depend on making a fundamental change in our culture and to the way our people understand their work and their responsibilities to their team and to the entire company. The long-term goal is to become even stronger as a knowledge-sharing culture—a culture that helps create value for Accenture and its stakeholders. Without that, even, the greatest technology infrastructure alone cannot make the difference."

- In a corporate environment, the traditional line between learning and knowledge sharing is becoming extremely difficult to draw. Learning and knowledge management solutions are blending, merging and beginning to look more like each other.
- Research has shown that large percentages of learning organizations are also overseeing related endeavors such as knowledge sharing and performance support.
- Underlying business changes are driving the integration of learning and knowledge management, because the marketplace and economic environment are changing so rapidly that organizations do not always have time for formal or traditional training design.
- Organizations that want to take advantage of synergies from integrated learning and knowledge management capabilities should put both initiatives under the same management oversight team.
- Creating better knowledge sharing capabilities helps an organization achieve at least three main goals: enhance revenue, create better efficiencies to drive out wasted time and excessive costs, and foster innovation.
- Employees actually spend relatively small percentages of their time in formal learning programs, so companies need to determine ways to reach employees with knowledge and learning wherever they are working, whenever the need it.
- The "just-in-time" approach to learning at the heart of a knowledge management and knowledge sharing strategy leads to more effective job performance and to greater retention of the knowledge and experience gained, so future performance of the same task will be even better.
- Organizations should not try to build the "perfect" knowledge management application right away. Instead, they

should get a working solution in production and then iterate based on real experience so that changes made will be based on how the system is actually being used.

- A knowledge sharing system must be designed from the perspective of those who will be using the system.

Nine

Learning and Value Creation: Accenture Looks to the Future

No matter how successful a transformational change program is, there is always one sobering fact to bear in mind: the journey is never over. Certainly there have been times when the Accenture team has been able to step back and celebrate its accomplishments. But there is little time to rest in such a competitive industry. Today, Accenture is moving on in its relentless quest for high performance, finding new ways to enable its global workforce, connect employees to each other, align their performance with business needs and give them an opportunity to bring their innovations to bear upon the success of the company.

One of the humbling, but also exciting, aspects of the fields of learning, knowledge management and workforce performance is that the more one works in these fields, the more one also realizes how much more there is to learn and do. Accenture has been a leader to date in delivering phenomenal learning experiences to its employees in order to boost business performance. Now, the company is also seeking out new ways to tap into the intelligence and experience of its workforce to create additional business value. Traditional training, after all, was mostly a one-way phenomenon: a course was created in a central group and then delivered to employees. Today, high-performance businesses also seek to get the flow of intellectual energy moving in the opposite direction, too. They know there is a tremendous latent resource in the individual and collaborative minds of their people, and they want to create a knowledge refinery that transforms that resource into additional value.

But the truth is, when you move from the relatively straightforward kind of cause and effect that distinguishes traditional training, and enter a dimension where your goal is tapping into the collective thinking of the workforce, then planning, design, management and measurement become exceedingly complex. With training, it's possible to create key performance indicators for individuals, measure those indicators before and after a training event, and then arrive at a fairly accurate idea of what effect the training has on business performance. But once you open up that simpler world of cause and effect to multiple individuals interacting in multiple kinds of ways with multiple kinds of content and experiences, the permutations can quickly multiply almost out of control.

Yet figuring out that complex calculus—how learning, leadership, workforce performance, knowledge capital and multiple other factors interrelate—is something that Accenture is now working to advance. Accenture's overall story here has been framed as a learning story, because that is where the primary energy was being generated. But if you zoom out from that focus, it's clear that reinventing learning for high performance takes place as part of a much larger picture of how organizations leverage people, ideas and communities for competitive advantage. This new world that Accenture is now helping to create is one in which organizations and their leaders become increasingly sophisticated at putting in place the right conditions for human value, intellectual value and social value to interact in order to create high performance and ever-greater value.

That new world is still a vision, of course: a future destination which, though compelling and carrying with it an air of inevitability, is far from being realized. The question for Accenture—and for all organizations today—is how to balance vision and reality. How can organizations move forward with the incremental steps necessary to create and reach this future destination, and arrive there with the robust economic and cultural health necessary to thrive?

Human capital and human value

The most obvious domain in which to place Accenture's learning reinvention program is in the area of human capital theory—a field growing more sophisticated each year thanks to ongoing research into the economic value of things like human thinking, learning and knowledge. The foundational work for human capital analysis was done about 40 years ago. Gary S. Becker, the Nobel prize-winning economist from the University of Chicago, created acceptance among a wider audience for the term "human capital" with his 1964 book of that name. The fact that serious economists were demonstrating the relationship between investments in people and economic growth was crucial to advancements in management thinking. And it was management visionary Peter Drucker who, in a series of books over several decades, helped to advance the idea that it was no longer tangible manufactured goods, or even services, but *knowledge itself* that would be the chief form of capital by the time the twenty-first century rolled around. He was right.

That kind of thinking has made it possible to move organizations and their leaders away from a mechanistic, Newtonian and simplistic view of what an organization is and does. Gradually, senior executives have been growing more comfortable with concepts like the "learning organization" and "intangible assets." These ideas indicate a growing recognition that an organization is not just hard assets of structural capital. There is value found in the people of an organization and in what they do.

A helpful concept here is a term which, though not new, has only fairly recently been added to the more common lexicon of terms like structural capital, human capital and intellectual/knowledge capital. It is "social capital," the value of the interrelationships within the community and culture of an organization. When companies like Accenture work to increase their capabilities in knowledge management, it's really social capital they're after: the difference between the value of one person's knowledge and the value of many people's knowledge, where the whole becomes greater than the sum of the parts.

Together, human capital (leaders and other workers), intellectual/knowledge capital (knowledge and information) and social capital (people and teams) interact to create value, but how exactly they do so, and how one might predict the value created from it, measure it and then encourage maximum production of that value remain great unknowns. Yet one can begin to see the outlines of how the kind of "return on learning" model developed by Accenture might one day be expanded to include the interactions of people to generate value.

If there is one particular addition or advancement related to this broader area of human capital transformation that the Accenture team believes it has made during its learning transformation journey, it has been its insistence on a broader understanding of how value is created for organizations today. It is *not* just a matter of manipulating human capital and intangible assets into organizational value. It is how the human value and the value of information and the value of relationships interact to produce organizational value. All of the detailed curricula planning, all of the work in creating phenomenal learning, state-of-the-art learning technologies and better governances—these were all, ultimately, a means of generating business outcomes.

Indeed, the new frontier in workforce performance is designing, managing and measuring organizations *with the outcome in mind,* not just a focus on the intermediate steps to that value. Says Craig Mindrum, part of Vanthournout's visioning team and someone who has worked over the past 20 years in the field of change management, "To say, after all, that people engage in 'knowledge work' is merely speaking of the materials people work with and manipulate, not necessarily the outcome that is produced. It is like calling a potter a 'clay worker' or an artist a 'paint worker.'"

Similarly, even though studies in areas like intangible assets, human capital and intellectual capital are fascinating and important, they are, again, rooted in the value of the materials being manipulated. What is needed is a model, and then an architectural framework, that will allow leaders to design and execute a business according to the outcome—the *value*—being created by the people and the "stuff" they are working with: structural assets, human value, and intellectual value. Says Mindrum, "The late twentieth century was the era of knowledge work and knowledge workers. The first part of the twenty-first century will be about 'value work' and 'value workers.'"

The choice of words used to speak of how organizations achieve high performance through workforce transformation is not merely a matter of semantics. The words indicate the sophistication of the thinking behind them. To be sure, if the objective is to measure and track the value of the assets of an organization, one can hardly do without concepts like "human capital." By becoming more sophisticated in human capital analysis and measurement, organizations can begin to differentiate their workforce strategies and create competitive advantage through their workforce capabilities. But valuable as the concept of human capital has been to economists, when it comes to actual interactions with the workforce and giving them what they need to create value for an organization, "human capital" is a phrase that describes an inert and abstract object, whose value increases or decreases by an organization's manipulation of it. This mindset has been very difficult for business people and academic thinkers alike to shed—another example of the simplistic, mechanistic organizational mindset discussed earlier. It's not human capital that organizations are working with; it's people. Human capital is an abstraction; it can't generate better business performance. But real people and real teams can.

Learning and knowledge management have a vital role to play in maximizing human, intellectual, social and organizational value. Learning professionals are deeply skilled in exactly what organizations now need more than ever: the ability to create individual excellence in performance more quickly and to help individuals adapt more rapidly to changing conditions (human value); to connect those individuals to others both inside and outside the organization in the quest for better ways to perform and to serve customers (social value); to manage the knowledge and experience in an organization and make advancements that occur in any part of a company immediately available to every other part (intellectual value); and to accelerate the benefits of collaboration and to harvest the fruits of collaboration and knowledge sharing as innovation and value creation (organizational value).

To stay ahead of the competition and to maximize the impact on the performance of its own workforce, Accenture is working in all these areas.

Bringing rigor to investments in an organization's workforce

The Accenture High-Performance Workforce Study, an exclusive and comprehensive survey of 244 executives in six countries, found that measuring the impact of human capital initiatives is not routine for most organizations. The study found that only 20 to 25 percent of respondents regularly and frequently measure critical areas such as manager and workforce proficiency, leadership capability and employee engagement; only 30 percent measure the time to competence of their critical workers.

It is not that executives lack the desire to bring rigor to their human capital investments. More often, they lack the tools and the knowledge they need to assess their current human capital capabilities and processes so they can set a more effective course toward the future.

What would be the ideal characteristics of an effective tool to guide human capital investments? Such a tool would help executives understand how human capital contributes to bottom-line financial results; it would determine optimal investment decisions; and it would measure the benefits and progress made from those investments, helping executives decide if they are on the right course, and helping them change course if necessary.

These characteristics are, in fact, the capabilities of the Accenture Human Capital Development Framework, developed by the Accenture Institute for High Performance Business in partnership with the Accenture Human Performance practice. With the Human Capital Development Framework, organizations can move beyond subjectivity and intuition, and manage their investments based on objective information. The Human Capital Development Framework enables organizations to diagnose their strengths and weaknesses in key human capital processes, benchmark their performance against others, and track performance changes over time. More importantly, the framework enables executives to assess their capacity to achieve superior business results through investments in human capital.

Based on objective data—collected from employees, business leaders, HR executives, and finance and HR information systems—the framework provides guidance to assess, benchmark and determine the relationships between elements at four distinct levels or tiers.

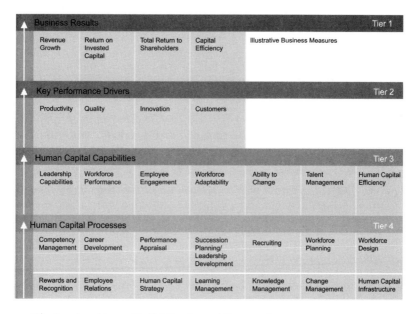

The Accenture Human Capital Development Framework

- **Business results**—the financial measures of organizational success.
- **Key performance drivers**—the intermediate organizational outcomes that typically are captured on a balanced scorecard.

- **Human capital capabilities**—the most immediate and visible people-related qualities that human capital processes produce.
- **Human capital processes**—the specific practices and activities that organizations undertake to develop their human capital capabilities.

Learning and knowledge management

To begin, notes Vanthournout, an important step is to continually increase the sophistication of the company's learning model to create deep skills in people that can be brought to bear anywhere around the global organization. "One of the things we had to reassert during our learning reinvention program over the past few years was the way learning can create a common base of experience in support of our culture. That had become broken. It's safe to say, one of the things we are proudest of is how a sense of commonality and shared values is being reinvigorated at Accenture. We regularly get course evaluations from our employees all over the world who speak of how vital the experience at the St. Charles campus was to them—learning from experienced senior executives at Accenture, and interacting with other bright minds from our far-flung practice. We also get feedback from more experienced employees—those who have been with the company for several years—who say that they had been thinking about leaving the company, but had come away from their experience here with renewed energy and purpose. 'Why would I ever want to leave a place like this?' they sometimes write, and that is not only enormously gratifying to us, but also important as our company strives to attract and retain the best talent in the world."

The next step for Accenture, however, is to build on the reinvigoration of the core curriculum and the common learning experiences to create even deeper skills in its workforce. This is part of an important business trend today: increasing the sophistication by which companies differentiate their employees, jobs and workforce management approaches, because these are advantages that cannot be imitated so readily by competitors. According to Jill Smart, "Our greatest achievements in recent years have been in enabling our people to have common learning experiences again, and in improving our ability to run learning like a business so we can offer our programs efficiently and at scale. But now we need to improve our capability to differentiate our people based on their knowledge and expertise. We want our employees to share a base of knowledge and experience, but now we also need to create deeper specialty skills in our people: depth of knowledge in industry areas and in functional or capability areas."

These areas of learning and experience are much more dynamic. So Accenture is looking to create a continuous learning environment where people can stay abreast of ever-changing markets. To a degree, this focus means giving up a bit of control over the learning environment—relying much more on people learning from each other through knowledge sharing than solely on learning coming from a centralized group. "To date," says Vanthournout, "to get both learning and knowledge management up and working at peak performance, we have been focusing on optimizing each of them fairly separately. Now, however, we are going to be thinking of them holistically so we can make wiser decisions about when to leverage learning, when to leverage knowledge management and when to leverage an approach where the distinction itself becomes irrelevant. Ultimately, one simply wants to deliver to employees whatever they need—call it a learning asset, call it a knowledge asset, call it whatever—to complete whatever tasks they have in front of them, whenever they need to perform those tasks."

Engaging the workforce

Just as it was an important signal to the global Accenture organization when learning and knowledge management were placed under the same leadership area—global HR under Jill Smart, and specifically under Vanthournout's capability development group—so another important signal has been sent to the practice by charging

Vanthournout and his team with the responsibility to improve "employee engagement" at Accenture. "What that means," says Vanthournout, "is that in an ideal situation, a company's learning group is not in business just to build skills. What we're about here is driving bottom-line business results, and bringing together a number of areas like learning and knowledge management to build skills, leverage knowledge and actively engage our people in their work for their benefit and the benefit of the company. One of the key lessons coming out of our entire experience with reinventing learning at Accenture has been that more CEOs need to be aware of the enormous potential they have to excel in the marketplace and differentiate themselves from competitors by taking an innovative but also business-oriented approach to accelerating the performance of their workforce through learning and knowledge management." (See box.)

Enterprise learning on the boardroom radar

One of the goals driving the entire learning transformation initiative at Accenture was to make enterprise learning one of the top three business objectives for Accenture's senior executives.

To an extent, that is every organization's goal today. To make that happen, organizations need to make an important shift in mindset, and look at the business *outcomes* that are now possible through enterprise learning and related initiatives in collaboration, knowledge management and performance support. Here are 10 broad categories of outcomes that C-level executives should be helping to drive from their enterprise learning capabilities.

1. Winning against the competition

Winning against the competition can result from many things, but two important ways to make it happen are through innovation and through better customer service. Many companies are discovering how advanced learning strategies and techniques can help them deliver in both those areas of competitive advantage, by ensuring that service agents create the kinds of customer experiences that build satisfaction and loyalty in the customer base.

2. Delivering top- and bottom-line results

Research by Accenture Learning has shown that high-performance learning organizations help deliver better revenue and profit growth compared to their competitors and industry peers. Companies with high-performance learning capabilities have:

- Productivity (as measured by sales per employee) that is 27 percent greater.
- Revenue growth that is 40 percent higher.
- Net income growth that is 50 percent greater.

3. Achieving enterprise performance improvement by optimizing the performance of the most critical workforces

Often, incremental performance improvements among three to five workforces, even in a complex and global company, can make a 10 to 15 percent difference in a company's top and bottom lines. By isolating a key performance factor for each critical workforce (for example, spending the most time with the most profitable customers, or cross-selling while addressing service inquiries) a company can quickly quantify the potential benefits and support those with better learning and knowledge management capabilities.

4. Improving performance at speed and scale

Companies that need to quickly move large numbers of people, often geographically dispersed, to higher levels of performance often find themselves hindered rather than helped by their existing training organization. Improved learning capabilities, aided by the right technologies, can deliver dramatic performance improvements even in support of a large-scale change initiative.

5. Enhancing workforce performance over time, cost-effectively

One issue organizations face when it comes to learning and knowledge management is that the technologies change so rapidly. It is often impossible to justify the cost of frequent changes in infrastructure, and often difficult to find skills internally to keep up with technology change. As the Accenture learning organization discovered, the intelligent use of outsourcing services can leverage expertise and deliver high-quality learning on time and on budget, with high impact on overall business results.

6. Aligning the workforce with strategy

It's not necessarily the companies with the best strategy that win; it's the companies whose workforces know how to execute in alignment with strategy. The learning function is vital to maintaining workforce alignment with strategy because it has, arguably, the most touchpoints of any function in today's global organizations. Learning is one important way that the board can deliver its messages about what is essential to corporate success, and ensure that up-to-date thinking can be assimilated into the way the workforce learns and works.

7. Increasing the capacity to innovate

Executives report that innovation is among the top 10 items on their organization's strategic agenda, yet few companies are putting in place the right processes and tools to harvest the intelligence of their workforces to create innovations. The learning function has an important role to play in making the connections that lead to growth and innovation. Innovative companies create an environment that fosters innovation as a way of being. And there is no other function with more capacity to change an enterprise's culture than the learning function.

8. Lowering the risks of non-compliance and unethical behavior

Recent high-profile cases have underscored the importance of effective training when it comes to compliance with regulations like Sarbanes-Oxley, as well as a host of issues covering ethical business practices. Executives increasingly are asking the learning function not just to document the percentage of people it has run through compliance training, but to show the extent to which the training is having an impact.

9. Lessening the negative impact of an aging workforce

The average age of the workforce in many countries is creeping up, and some industry sectors and geographies will begin to feel the impact of this demographic trend in as little as five to 10 years as higher percentages of workers retire. Companies in most industries face the prospect of having to do the same amount of work, and possibly more work, with fewer employees. Solutions and strategies that integrate learning and knowledge management will become vital if companies are to counter the impact of this knowledge and experience leaving the workforce.

10. Improving employee engagement and retention

The "war for talent" is heating up again in many industries, and executives must be increasingly attuned to how effectively they are attracting and retaining the workers necessary to succeed. Accenture research has found that organizations investing intelligently in learning have more engaged workforces. Organizations that perform the learning management process well—a process that includes meeting regularly with a mentor or advisor to review learning needs and develop a learning plan—have significantly higher employee engagement than organizations that perform it poorly.

The issue of employee engagement is increasingly important to executives today, as surveys have found that high percentages of employees from many industries are actively disengaged from their work and their companies. A disengaged workforce spells trouble for companies in both good economic times and bad. In a slow economy, retention may be high, but a disengaged workforce operates at low levels of productivity. In a recovering economy, the loss of talent caused by low engagement can have a serious impact on business results. On the positive side, research has found that higher levels of engagement not only improve retention, but drive up customer satisfaction, productivity and total shareholder return. In other words, high-performance businesses have an actively engaged workforce.

To ask if employees are engaged means going beyond "satisfaction" surveys, though these have their place. Engagement means that people are committed to improving business results through their work and that their performance actually does create value in ways they can feel and see.

How is Accenture scoring when it comes to engagement? "What our people are telling us today," says Vanthournout, "is that we are very good at spelling out the processes that affect our workforce. When it comes to career development, for example, our people know what we have in place and they know where they fit in. Where we need to do a better job is in the personal relationships among leaders and employees: the coaching, the mentoring, the small things that go beyond the processes and actively help people navigate through those processes and structures." Several decades ago, writer and futurist John Naisbitt popularized the phrase "high-tech and high-touch" to describe what companies need in order to grow—and that describes one of Accenture's challenges. Says Vanthournout, "The advancements we've made in bringing technology to bear on our learning and knowledge sharing have been extraordinary. Now, those advancements need to be matched by high-touch capabilities. The greatest impact executives can have on their organizations today is by improving the manner with which they interact with employees—drawing them into the work of the organization and letting them know that their individual contributions matter."

In a sense, this brings Vanthournout's team full circle...back to the principles by which they planned and executed the entire learning reinvention program at Accenture, according to the leadership model introduced in Chapter 2. The model emphasizes three leadership roles in particular: business operators, value creators and people developers. "Historically," says Vanthournout, "we have been world-class when it comes to developing leaders who are business operators and value creators. Today, we have a renewed focus on building leaders who are also world-class at helping our people to grow and thrive."

Accenture expects learning to take a more visible role in improving employee engagement. Consider the issue of "phenomenal learning." There, Accenture had leveraged its understanding of the importance of the "experience economy" to engage employees along four different dimensions: the learning experience, networking, enculturation and the guest experience—surprising and delighting learners by the quality, engagement and even festive nature of the time spent in the classroom. Today, Kurt Olson is pushing to include employee engagement considerations in how learning is planned, designed and delivered. "In addition to everything else we have done to deliver phenomenal learning to our people," says Olson, "we now want to make sure that when they leave one of our classes, they feel that a senior executive who has served as faculty has connected with them personally. We want them to understand and fully buy into how that course will help them serve our clients better, and how it will help them progress professionally. Above all, we want our people to walk away from a class feeling really proud that they work for this company, right now, right here."

Getting employee engagement right requires keeping the proper end in mind. Craig Mindrum sees an important linkage between engaging employees and helping them become "value workers." "Organizations need to be working to improve employee engagement not only because of its effect on retention. If that's the only driver, companies will not achieve the long-term results that help them achieve high performance. What inevitably happens is that efforts to improve engagement will wax strong when the economy is good—when employees have more job options and companies are scrambling to retain the best workers—and then will wane when the economy weakens. Where I see Accenture going is using learning, knowledge management and leadership development to increase the involvement of their employees—their 'value workers'—and tapping into their collective intelligence. Yes, engagement will improve; yes, retention will improve; but the main driver is improving the contribution of employees and the value they help to create. Better retention is a byproduct, not the primary goal; retention will improve naturally as people feel they are more closely linked to the core value-creating process of the company."

The changing landscape of learning technologies

The Accenture team also is looking into how some of the newer learning technologies available today—MP3 players (for so-called "podcasting" and "vodcasting"), blogging, gaming and the like—can have an impact on how learning is delivered: its effectiveness, its ability to blend in more seamlessly with people's lives and its cost-effectiveness. John Ceisel notes, "Many of these newer learning technologies can help drive high performance for organizations that can embrace them more quickly and apply them to the right business objectives. For example, podcasting and vodcasting bring several distinct advantages to enterprise learning: mobility, speed-of-content capture and distribution, and the ability to bring relevant learning experiences to a large audience in a cost-effective manner." Dan Bielenberg, who joined Vanthournout's team to help drive many of these technologies into Accenture's learning approach, adds, "Many of these technologies can help us create a more engaging learning environment for the 'digital natives' coming into the workforce—the twentysomethings who grew up using these technologies almost as second nature."

A powerful effect on how people work

In the end, the Accenture team can look at the impact of its work to reinvent learning and see a palpable effect on the culture of the company, and on how its more than 126,000 employees live and work. These employees now have more immediate access to the learning and knowledge assets they need, through the myLearning system. They understand the curriculum that has been created to help them grow. They can more easily search for information and expertise that helps them address specific learning and performance needs as they arise. They can arrive at the central St. Charles campus to work, learn and socialize with colleagues from all around the globe. Or, they can take a virtual class from anywhere in the world—in real time or as a recorded session that they can access at their convenience.

Says Vanthournout, "The effects of our learning transformation program at Accenture have gone well beyond learning. Today, we are helping to connect truly global teams through our learning and knowledge management technologies. We've always been a global company, of course, but in reality, that usually meant putting together teams located in different parts of the world. Today, it's a rare exception to be on a work team that does not involve collaborating with other employees across time zones and across geographies."

Beyond the immediate effects of learning that are easiest to see and experience are a host of other, less tangible effects. Accenture has stepped up to fulfill the promise it makes to those who join the company: to commit to their professional development; to give them world-class opportunities in both work and learning; to commit to their growth in both good economic times and bad. And there is growing pride throughout the organization as Accenture wins more awards and recognition for its work in learning and knowledge management. This external validation is additional assurance that things are moving in the right direction.

Accenture's awards today carry significance beyond what the

company did 25 years ago, when the emphasis was primarily on the quality of the courses themselves. Today, although the learning itself is still of "phenomenal" quality, the awards acknowledge how effectively Accenture is using learning to drive toward high performance.

And that should be of interest to every one of a company's stakeholders—including its shareholders. The return on learning is good for an organization: good for its people and good for its leadership. Ultimately, though, it's good for business.

- As companies move forward to realize a new vision for learning and knowledge management, they should focus on differentiating their workforces—creating deep skills in people that can be brought to bear anywhere around the organization.
- Organizations should now be thinking of learning and knowledge management holistically so they can make wiser decisions about when to leverage learning, when to leverage knowledge management and when to leverage an approach where the distinction itself becomes irrelevant.
- The new frontier in management today is designing, managing and measuring organizations with a focus on the value outcome in mind, not just on the intermediate steps to that value.
- The late twentieth century was the era of knowledge work and knowledge workers. The first part of the twenty-first century will be about "value work" and "value workers."
- Human value, intellectual value, social value and structural assets all combine to create organizational value. In the future, financial models will become more sophisticated in their ability to depict how all of these components interact.
- Employee engagement increasingly is an issue for companies in search of high performance. The learning function can make a huge difference to the engagement of people in their work.
- A company's learning group is not in business just to build skills. It is there to drive bottom-line business results, bringing together a number of areas like learning and knowledge management to build skills, leverage knowledge and actively engage people in their work for their benefit and the benefit of the company.
- The greatest impact executives can have today on their organizations is in improving the manner with which they interact with employees—drawing them into the work of the organiza-

tion and letting them know that their individual contributions matter.

- Increasing the engagement of employees is important not
  only to retaining them and improving productivity. It is
  important to growth and innovation—tapping into the collective intelligence of value workers.

ACKNOWLEDGMENTS

Given the size and scope of Accenture, the learning transformation initiative described in this book owes its success to the vision, commitment and hard work of literally hundreds of people throughout the world. First and foremost, we thank the people of Accenture, whose commitment to their personal growth, and the growth of the company, is unparalleled in the industry. More specifically, the authors wish to acknowledge the special contribution of the following:

The Capability Development Executive Steering Committee, for the sponsorship that made it possible to revitalize training and maximize the return on learning at Accenture: Tim Breene, Martin Cole, Joellin Comerford, Karl-Heinz Floether, Mark Foster, Gill Rider, Stephen Rohleder, Basilio Rueda, Scott Sargent, Jill Smart, David Thomlinson and Diego Visconti.

The Solution Planning team, for making phenomenal learning a reality every day at Accenture and for creating exceptional curricula for our knowledge workers around the globe: Anne Aiello, Alycia Bavero, Jennifer Black, Amy Bouque, Richard Busby, Lisa Callahan, Dan Dupre, Susan Ford, Robert Gerard, Caroline Glasser, David Granger, Carolyn Henning, Allison Horn, Melissa Hurst, Jill Jackson, Virginia Kempiners, MaryAnn Kennedy, Charles Lagemann, Melissa Noonan, Clare Norman, Christopher Olson, Gregory Overley, Fiona Paulius, Whitney Paulowsky, Mary Carole Prasse, Beth Ruddock, Heber Sambucetti, Timothy Seidler and Christina Wolf.

The Capability Infrastructure team, for imagining, planning and managing a world-class learning infrastructure and for their commitment to keeping it running for all our people around the world: Tara Bryja, Dawn Hudspeth, Monica LaRosa, Richard

Ledone, Deborah Martin, Mary McDowell, Brandt Sartell and Michelle Smith.

The Capability Development Strategy team, for creating the vision of learning for business impact: Daniel Bielenberg, Brad Kolar, Maeve Lucas, Amanda Lutz, Kathryn McGregor, James Nolte, Brian Pugliese and Montgomery Watkins.

The Training Operations Management team, for delivering world-class training throughout the world: John DeCardy, Kelly Gismondo, Timothy Hobbs, Cindi Ingraham, Joseph Kotey, Elizabeth Mandernach, Kristin Martinez, Mary Matison, Liza Nguyen, Pat Santa, Allyson Sindone, Suzanne Snyder, Nancy Varela and Keith Worthington.

The Global Knowledge Management team, for creating and running a knowledge management system that is at the frontier of knowledge sharing: Susan Baktis, Steven Berzins, Stacie Jordan and Alessandra Maurilli.

The Performance Measurement team, for research and measurement excellence: Bruce Aaron, Diane Byars, Sarah Kimmel, Jerry Prochazka and Rachael Sheldrick.

And the other teams whose help has been essential to our success: the Capability Development Leads, the Training Operating Model team, the Knowledge Management Advisory Board and Accenture Learning.

ABOUT THE AUTHORS

Don Vanthournout is Accenture's chief learning officer. In his current role, he is in charge of the capability development needs, including learning and knowledge management, of the company's more than 126,000 employees located in more than 48 countries. After graduating from Bradley University in 1981 with a B.S. in mathematics and secondary education, with a business minor, he joined Accenture and spent almost 15 years working with external clients, before moving into a series of director-level roles in the company's learning organization. In 2001, he became the head of Accenture's Capability Development organization, and was subsequently named chief learning officer. He is very active with the local schools and youth sports programs in his community and his church.

Kurt Olson is director of capability solutions for Accenture, overseeing the curriculum planning activities for Accenture's employees worldwide. He earned a B.S. in computer science from Illinois State University and an M.B.A from Northern Illinois University, and is currently pursuing a Ph.D. in organization development from Benedictine University. The majority of his 20-year career with Accenture has been spent working in the learning industry. He has a patent pending for the "phenomenal learning" methodology that Accenture developed to support their learning analysis/design/development process. In addition, he is a Six Sigma Black Belt. His inspiration comes from his wife, Shelly, and their sons Michael and Connor.

John Ceisel is a senior manager in Accenture's Capability Development organization. He leads the team responsible for Accenture's new joiner orientation, consulting workforce core, as well as corporate compliance, sales effectiveness and professional development training. His prior roles at the company include being the business architect who drove myLearning's initial business requirements, and 10 years as a consultant working with external clients. He holds a B.A. in computer science from St. Joseph's College and an M.A. in learning sciences from Northwestern University. He is active in the community teaching and serving on local school and community boards, pursuing his personal mission "to impact the learning of my children's children." He is blessed with his wife, Jaikie, and their children Jennie, Katy and Chris.

Andrew White is the director of global training operations for Accenture. He earned a B.A. in economics from Duke University and an M.B.A. from the University of Michigan. He joined what was then the administrative services division of Arthur Andersen, later to become Accenture, in 1977 as a line consultant. White has since worked in Accenture's internal global education program for the past 20 years in a variety of roles. He is married to Betsy and is the proud father of one son, Drew, and the proud stepfather of one son, Stephen.

Tad Waddington is director of performance measurement for Accenture. He earned his B.A. in psychology at Arizona State University before going on to earn an M.A. in the history of religions from the Divinity School at the University of Chicago and a Ph.D. in measurement, evaluation and statistical analysis from the education department at the University of Chicago. He also worked as a research director for Gallup before joining Accenture in 1997. He is married to Yoko Miyamoto and they have one son, Elias.

Tom Barfield is director for the global knowledge management capabilities for Accenture, including the company's global knowledge management strategy and the infrastructure that drives that strategy. He joined Accenture after earning a B.S. in industrial engineering from Bradley University in 1991. His primary focus is on connecting the people of Accenture to the knowledge and learning assets they need to better serve their customers. He has a patent on leveraging virtual reality environments to convey abstract concepts. He and his wife, Lynda, have three children: Emily, Ryan and Kaelyn.

Samir Desai is a senior manager at Accenture and the product manager for myLearning, Accenture's internal learning management system. As such, he is responsible for the development and operations of Accenture's learning infrastructure. He earned a B.S. in electrical engineering from the University of Illinois Champaign-Urbana and an M.S. in computer science from Northwestern University. His passion in life is teaching and he has spent a majority of his career at Accenture in the learning industry. He himself learns about life from his wife, Bhavini, and their children, Karishma, Kaveen and Keyana.

Craig Mindrum is currently a visiting research fellow for Accenture Learning. Over a 25-year career as a consultant, researcher, writer and a college professor at DePaul and Indiana universities, he has focused on areas of human performance and organizational change, including communications, leadership and the moral design of organizations. Following master's work at Yale University and Indiana University, he received his Ph.D. from the University of Chicago. A senior contributing editor for *Outlook* magazine, his writing has appeared in numerous periodicals, and this is the fifth book he has either authored or co-authored. He and his wife, Donna, have three children: Jonathan, Jennifer and Jessica.